MARTHA STEWART'S WEDDING CAKES

Martha Stewart's

WEDDING CAKES

BY MARTHA STEWART

WITH WENDY KROMER

CLARKSON POTTER/PUBLISHERS

NEW YORK

{OPPOSITE} A close-up look at design details inspired by dressmakers' handiwork and "appliquéd" on a cake (also shown on page 82). On the following page is a romantic cake spilling over with white Swiss meringue hydrangea blossoms.

Some photographs and recipes originally
appeared in *Martha Stewart Weddings* magazine.

Library of Congress Cataloging-in-Publication Data
Stewart, Martha.
    Martha Stewart's wedding cakes / Martha Stewart with Wendy Kromer. — 1st ed.
    1. Wedding cakes. I. Kromer, Wendy. II. Title. III. Title: Wedding cakes.
TX771.S76 2007
641.8'653—dc22   2007014928

ISBN 978-0-307-39453-8

Printed in Spain

Design by Brooke Hellewell Reynolds

10 9 8 7 6 5 4 3 2 1

First Edition

THIS BOOK IS FOR EVERY BRIDE AND GROOM,
PAST, PRESENT, AND FUTURE, AND FOR EVERY
BAKER, FLORAL DESIGNER, CATERER, AND WEDDING PLANNER
WHO HELPS THEM PLAN THEIR PERFECT WEDDING.

—*Martha*

TO MY MOTHER, JOAN, AND AUNT EVELYN.
YOUR CREATIVITY, GRACE, AND LOVE FOR
ALL THINGS BEAUTIFUL CONTINUE TO INSPIRE.
TO MARTHA, FOR BELIEVING IN ME.

—*Wendy*

contents

INTRODUCTION 9

PORTRAIT OF A CAKE DESIGNER 10

CHOOSING YOUR CAKE
13

ALBUM OF CAKES
45

MAKING A WEDDING CAKE
203

SOURCES 254   ACKNOWLEDGMENTS 256

PHOTOGRAPH CREDITS 257

INDEX 258

INTRODUCTION
BY MARTHA STEWART

MY FIRST BIG CATERING JOB, IN THE EARLY 1970s, was a wedding for three hundred people in Darien, Connecticut. My cooking partner and I labored over the menu, the food, and the design of the wedding cake. I was the more adept pastry chef, having practiced on numerous birthday cakes for my daughter; I had experimented with great cake recipes and Swiss and Italian meringue frostings, flavorful fillings, and piping techniques and decorative elements. I elected to make a tiered cake and suggested to the bride and her mother that it be gâteau à l'orange (orange almond cake), with a creamy white Italian meringue frosting piped in a basketweave and decorated with pink and apricot old-fashioned roses from my garden. I had to purchase an air conditioner and a large professional refrigerator for this job, and I remember as if it were yesterday starting to assemble and decorate the cake at 9:30 p.m. the day before the wedding, which would take place at 4 o'clock. That long, long, night, I invented many of my techniques: chopstick spacers, a unique basketweave design, and bamboo skewer inserts to keep the tiers from sliding, to name just a few. Everything worked— the tiers of the cake were moist and flavorful and dense, the

icing smooth and creamy, and most important, the exact right texture for piping, and the architecture very workable.

Despite extremely hot weather and threatening thunderstorms, the wedding went off without a hitch and the food and cake were devoured by all. I was elated that our first big job was a success, and I started to book wedding after wedding, insisting that we could make all the food, provide the service, and of course create the cake.

Over the years I added lots of flavors of cakes and myriad decorative designs to my repertoire. I cannot tell you how many cakes I have made since then, but it must be in the many hundreds. I rarely changed my schedule and always preferred baking the layers a couple of days in advance and decorating the stacked tiers the night before, allowing the cake time to absorb the flavors and chill through and through before being transported to the final destination.

Many of my favorites are illustrated and discussed in this wonderful compilation of the great cakes that have appeared in *Martha Stewart Weddings* over the years. Enjoy looking through them all—and maybe even baking some!

{WEDDING MEMORIES} *I have several fabric-covered boards in my homes where I love to put photographs and memorabilia. This one has images from some favorite weddings, including those of my friend Charlotte Beers (far left, bottom), who had her celebratory lunch at my house in Maine; my beautiful employee and friend Page Marchese (far left, top), who was married on Martha's Vineyard; and Susan Magrino (bottom right), my friend and publicist for almost thirty years, whose fabulous wedding weekend in the Bahamas was amazingly well designed. I was an active participant in each of these events, contributing flowers or homemade cakes. The madeleine cake (center) I'm making here with Wendy and our* Weddings *editorial director, Darcy Miller, is shown on page 158. When my mother married (top right), she looked lovely in rust silk velvet.*

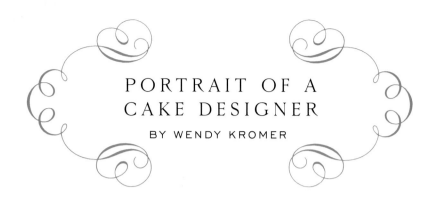

PORTRAIT OF A CAKE DESIGNER

BY WENDY KROMER

MY MOM WAS AN EXCELLENT COOK, BUT AS THE mother of six children, she rarely found the time to bake. That's where I came in. With Mom nearby, I became quite the princess of desserts in my house. However, as much as I enjoyed baking, I wanted more. I wanted to decorate my desserts and make them pretty. That's where my Aunt Evelyn came in.

If I was the princess of desserts, then Aunt Evelyn was the queen of cakes. Her wedding cakes were nothing short of breathtaking. When I was lucky enough to be invited to a wedding, I was mesmerized by the cake, by how delicious, fluffy, white frosting could create such pretty pearls, shells, and roses.

I did not grow up wanting to become a cake decorator, however. I wanted to be in fashion (again, there's that need to create and work with pretty things). After college, I visited an aunt and uncle living in Paris. Two weeks into my trip I knew I had to stay. To support myself, I turned to modeling. With modeling came travel—different cultures and their art, architecture, and cuisine. After ten years abroad, I *had* to get back to my first love—baking. So I retired from modeling (at the ripe old age of thirty-two) and immersed myself in professional pastry and baking studies at Peter Kump's New York

Cooking School (now the Institute of Culinary Education). My life experiences gave me insights into what taste could be, not only to the palate but to the eye. Inspiration comes in a variety of forms: the beauty of the fabric in a Japanese kimono, photographs of intricately detailed acanthus leaves, and architectural details I discovered during my travels.

With each bride and groom, my goal is to learn what is important to them for their wedding. I love to hear how they met, how and where they got engaged. Everyone has a story, and that story is revealed when I get to know the couple. The wedding venues, caterer, and florist, combined with the couple's personalities and a color palette or theme, help me understand their vision for their wedding day. Then I am able to start sketching ideas for their cake.

Initially, I was nervous when the editors at *Martha Stewart Living* called (in 1995) to ask me to work on a wedding cake with them. But I quickly learned we were all on the same quest: to create beautiful wedding cakes that would never go out of style. In this book you will find many of the cakes that I and other bakers have created over the past twelve years. I hope you will find them to be inspirational.

{STORY BOARD} *There I am celebrating my seventh birthday, and later my wedding, at which I served miniature pies instead of a cake. The pink ribbon is the one I use to wrap boxes; the logo was inspired by the old-fashioned powder-puff case. A piece of candy or a vintage monogram design can spark an idea. The monogram fondant hearts, first created for the cupcake tower (page 83), continue to be popular. Cherished items include letters I have received from clients, such as Darcy's thoughtful thank-you note, complete with a drawing of her cake (among her many talents, Darcy is also a brilliant illustrator). As for the postcard of my town, it just makes me smile.*

choosing your cake

FINDING INSPIRATION

14

A CAKE'S COMPONENTS

24

PRESENTING THE CAKE

33

PARTNERING WITH A PROFESSIONAL

40

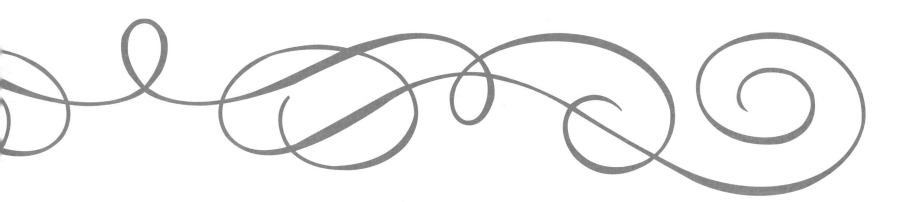

{ROSE TOPPER CAKE} *The beauty of this cake by Ron Ben-Israel is punctuated by the simplicity of a single flawless rose. The tiers are decorated with confectionary bands inspired by the lace of a bridal gown.*

A wedding cake is much more than dessert. It's a focal point at the event, a work of art, and a sweet symbol of a couple's love. As such, it should be as distinctive as the bride and groom themselves. A talented designer will help you develop ideas and then bake a memory to last a lifetime.

FINDING INSPIRATION

FEW DECISIONS ARE AS DELIGHTFUL AS CHOOSING your wedding cake. After all, what could be better than sampling bite after bite of delicious cake, plus frostings and fillings? But as eager as you may be to start meeting with bakers and tasting cakes, you'll get the best results if you do a little planning first. If you've set up a wedding binder or notebook, be sure to designate a section for inspiring cake pictures, plus notes on cakes you taste at other people's weddings. Ideally, you should order the cake six months before the wedding, so it's best to start considering what you want soon after you've chosen the time, date, and place for your reception.

To get a sense of what you like visually, start by perusing our album of cakes (pages 44 to 201) and collecting photographs from magazines and the Internet. If you find something that strikes your fancy, ask yourself what, exactly, you like about that particular cake. Is it the way the tiers appear to be floating? Or that they are hexagonal instead of round? Do you prefer the porcelain-smooth surface of a cake covered in fondant, the luscious look of buttercream, or the more playful swirls of meringue? Perhaps you're drawn to cakes that cascade with fresh flowers, or are a particular shade of yellow. The more familiar you are with what makes one cake different from another, the better you can express what you envision for your own cake.

The location, date, and time of your reception, as well as the overall feeling and style of the event, can all have their influence on the cake. As you plan and discover your preferences, think about how you might tie the look of the cake to your particular reception, as in the examples that follow.

{BEAUTIFUL BERRIES} *The just-ripening strawberries in this sunny cake are molded from white-chocolate "dough." Blossoms are made from gum paste, and the swags of tiny leaves are piped white-chocolate ganache.*

Wild Strawberry Cake
for 50

WEDDING STYLE

MODERN

{MODERN} *Square tiers covered in buttercream are striking in their simplicity. Lines of piped buttercream resemble strands of pearls. Velvety red rose petals make an understated topper to this cake by Cornerstone Caterers in Rye, New York.*

{TRADITIONAL} *Five fondant-covered tiers in varying heights and shapes are embellished with intricate royal icing piping and white chocolate rosettes in this classic confection.*

{RUSTIC} *On this tiramisu cake by Susan Spungen, chewy almond wafers are stacked with mascarpone cream and raspberries, then garnished with berry brambles and wild rose hips.*

{WHIMSICAL} *This playful cake by Wendy Kromer and Bill Yosses of Washington, D.C., was inspired by Neapolitan ice cream. The colors of chocolate, vanilla, and strawberry cover the outside in exuberant fondant dots, stripes, and a quilted pattern.*

RUSTIC

WHIMSICAL

SEASON

{SPRING} *The tangled stems of realistic, blushing gum-paste dogwood blooms scramble over white fondant tiers for a cake, designed by Wendy Kromer and Susan Spungen, that evokes the fresh feeling of spring.*

{SUMMER} *Piped in a ruffly basketweave pattern, these tiers resemble baskets brimming with summer's luscious strawberries, red currants, gooseberries, raspberries, and blueberries.*

{FALL} *Autumn leaves made from white chocolate and clusters of caramel-coated grapes make this buttercream cake, by Claire Perez, fitting for fall. See page 230 for leaf how-to.*

{WINTER} *Sculptural bare birch twigs, their tips wrapped in floral tape, circle fondant-covered tiers to mimic a frost-covered forest. Diminutive gum-paste birds search for treats: flecks of vanilla bean that flavor the "snow."*

SUMMER

FALL

WINTER

LOCATION

{WOODLAND} *For this nature-inspired cake, smooth buttercream-frosted tiers are piped with green buttercream ferns, then adorned with acorns and oak leaves from the garden.*

{GARDEN} *A cheery flower-filled reception deserves an equally cheery cake. This one, made of three fondant tiers, is topped with an initial made of hand-painted sugar-paste flowers; several more buds are dotted along the bottom of each tier.*

{TROPICS} *Fondant bands inspired by the interlaced loops of handwoven Puerto Rican furniture wrap the five tiers of this lofty confection by Lourdes Padilla of Puerto Rico. Exotic-looking orchids between tiers spill over the sides of the cake.*

{SEASIDE} *Ideal for a wedding on a boat or near a marina, this towering four-tier cake by Sandee Mortensen is covered with buttercream and decorated with colorful white-chocolate nautical flags.*

WOODLAND

TROPICS

SEASIDE

MOTIF

{COLOR} *This fondant-covered cake by Cheryl Kleinman could be a bride's "something blue" or a detail in a wedding with an overall blue-and-white color palette. The six square tiers are piped with "lace swatches" in royal icing.*

{FABRIC} *Delicate fondant "ribbons" are tied into the smart bows that march down the pastel tiers of this cake, inspired by Christian Dior's 1947 "New Look" designs. Edible decorations can mimic fabric from the bride's dress or the ribbon used to tie her bouquet.*

{FLOWERS} *A four-tier cake by Vosges Haut-Chocolat is topped with a bountiful cluster of lush peonies. More pink petals decorate the four corners of the square tiers.*

{FRUIT} *White chocolate grapes and sugar-paste leaves spill over the tiers of this fondant-covered cake. Royal-icing trellises create the illusion of a larger cake and hide the supporting dowels.*

FLOWERS

FRUIT

Most wedding cakes are made up of four basic elements: the cake layers, the filling between them, the icing or other decorative coating, and any embellishments. As focused as you may be on the cake's exterior, you will also want to savor the experience of creating delicious flavor combinations.

A CAKE'S COMPONENTS

A CAKE'S LOVELINESS SHOULD NOT BE MERELY frosting-deep. What you eat should be as delightful as what you see. Do you have a particular childhood favorite, such as devil's food or strawberry shortcake? Odds are, it will be even better when stacked several tiers tall. Or start with classic flavor combinations, such as caramel and apple, or those that are more novel—say, pistachio and white chocolate. The time of year can provide inspiration as well. Pears and apples feel right in the fall, berries and apricots in the summer. Cake layers flecked with nuts and spices feel warm and wintry; a tangy buttermilk cake tastes as fresh as springtime. Of course you could also let your menu spark your creativity. A Mediterranean-style dinner might inspire an orange-flavored cake, while an Asian feast could end with a cake featuring ginger.

As you think about flavors, consider how the cake will look sliced and plated. You could have three different cake layers filled with the same filling, or the same cake layers spread with three different fillings. Also think about texture: Replacing one of the cake layers with a baked meringue disk adds an unexpected element of crispness; crushed praline adds crunch to creamy fillings.

Ultimately you will want to take your baker's advice as to the best combinations and the proper use of ingredients. Delicate fruits such as raspberries, for example, are best paired with a white or almond cake and an icing that isn't too rich. An airy sponge cake works best with a light mousse or buttercream filling. A rich, dense chocolate cake could have a light filling for contrast, or a luscious one (such as bittersweet ganache) for a more decadent result.

{NEAPOLITAN SLICE} *The familiar flavors and colors of strawberry, chocolate, and vanilla appear in this cake's layers, the fillings of strawberry jam and ganache, and the fondant coating.*

CAKES

{NO. 1} ALMOND DACQUOISE

{NO. 2} COCONUT

{NO. 3} WHITE BUTTER

{NO. 4} MOIST YELLOW

{NO. 5} ALMOND-CORNMEAL POUND CAKE

{NO. 6} LEMON POPPY SEED POUND CAKE

{NO. 7} ALMOND HAZELNUT

{NO. 8} CARROT

{NO. 9} APPLE

{NO. 10} MARBLE

{NO. 11} RED VELVET

{NO. 12} DEVIL'S FOOD

{NO. 13} CHOCOLATE BUTTER CAKE

{NO. 14} MOCHA SPICE

FROSTINGS
AND FILLINGS

{NO. 1} VANILLA-BEAN BUTTERCREAM

{NO. 2} CREAM CHEESE FROSTING

{NO. 3} CARAMEL–CREAM CHEESE FILLING

{NO. 4} PISTACHIO BUTTERCREAM

{NO. 5} CHOCOLATE BUTTERCREAM

{NO. 6} CHOCOLATE-CHERRY GANACHE

{NO. 7} CARAMEL FILLING

{NO. 8} FUDGE FROSTING

{NO. 9} PASTRY CREAM

{NO. 10} APRICOT FILLING

{NO. 11} SWISS MERINGUE BUTTERCREAM

{NO. 12} COCONUT BUTTERCREAM

{NO. 13} WHITE CHOCOLATE MOUSSE

{NO. 14} SEEDLESS RASPBERRY JAM

{NO. 15} COFFEE BUTTERCREAM

{NO. 16} VANILLA CUSTARD BUTTERCREAM
(TINTED PINK)

{NO. 17} LEMON CURD

{NO. 18} SEVEN-MINUTE FROSTING

1

2

3

4

5

6

7

8

9

10

11

12

13

14

15

16

17

18

{CAKE TASTING}

When you visit a baker, you may be offered a selection of small portions similar to these. Try bites of the different cakes, frostings, and fillings together, so you'll know how they'll work in the finished creation.

ICINGS AND MORE

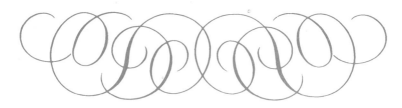

There are many ways to decorate a cake. The various icings and edible trimmings used to give a dessert its distinct appearance and flavor all have their own unique qualities. It will be easiest to determine what you want if you know all your options. Plus, you'll feel more at ease when you meet with a baker if you know the terminology.

BUTTERCREAM

{ DESCRIPTION }

This soft, satiny frosting—essentially a meringue blended with a generous amount of butter—can be spread over a cake, piped into patterns, or used as a creamy filling. Buttercream can easily be flavored and tinted any color. As it is neither too heavy nor too sweet, this frosting complements cakes without overpowering them.

{ SPECIAL CONSIDERATIONS }

A cake covered or filled with buttercream must be kept refrigerated, then brought to room temperature just before serving. Because the frosting melts easily, it's not ideal for an outdoor wedding, especially if the cake will be displayed in direct sunlight.

CHOCOLATE MODELING DOUGH

{ DESCRIPTION }

This is melted chocolate mixed with corn syrup until pliable, like a dough. Rolled out and cut, it is ideal for forming bands to wrap around a cake's layers. It dries to a firm consistency, so it is also excellent for making delicate flowers.

{ SPECIAL CONSIDERATIONS }

Since it contains more chocolate than chocolate-flavored fondant, the modeling dough has a more pronounced taste. As with any chocolate, it is sensitive to heat and humidity. Once dried, it can be brittle; make sure your baker makes more than enough in case of breakage and packages the decorative shapes very carefully.

COMPOTES/FRUIT GLAZES/PRESERVES

{ DESCRIPTION }

Compotes, preserves, and glazes are all made from fruit, sugar, and water. Compotes are simmered until the fruit is soft but maintains its shape. Continue to cook the mixture for preserves. For a glaze, preserves are heated, then strained. Compotes and preserves are used as filling; glazes can be an undercoat for frosting or can be used alone for a finish with sheen.

{ SPECIAL CONSIDERATIONS }

Depending on the fruit used to make them, preserves and compotes can discolor light-colored frosting and cake layers. Glazes can help keep cakes fresh by sealing in moisture.

CURD

{ DESCRIPTION }

A curd is a fruit spread enriched with egg yolks and butter, with a texture similar to that of pudding. When still warm, it can be poured as a glaze. When chilled, it can be spread over the tops of finished cake tiers or between cake layers as a filling. Curds pair especially well with pound cakes and dacquoise. Lemon is the most traditional curd flavor, but virtually any fruit can flavor a curd.

{ SPECIAL CONSIDERATIONS }

Once chilled, curds need to stay cool, so they shouldn't be used on cakes too big to be refrigerated. The eggs in a curd are cooked enough so that safety is not a concern, provided the curd is kept chilled until ready to serve.

DECORATIVE CHOCOLATE

{ DESCRIPTION }

Large blocks of chocolate can be skimmed with a sharp knife (or other tool) to create delicate curls; chopped and melted to use for piping patterns on the cake; or tempered (a process that gives chocolate more sheen) to make molded shapes. (See page 229 for how to temper chocolate.) To ensure the finest texture and flavor, the highest quality chocolate should be used.

{ SPECIAL CONSIDERATIONS }

Chocolate can be hard to work with. It doesn't fare well in extreme temperatures (it will melt if it gets too hot) or humidity (it might sweat, especially after being stored at cooler temperatures). If you'd like a cake decorated with chocolate, consider the temperature at your reception site, as well as the potential weather on your wedding day.

FONDANT

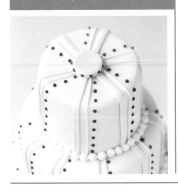

{ DESCRIPTION }

When rolled out and draped over tiers, this smooth, firm sugar icing makes a stable surface for appliqués, gum-paste flowers, or royal-icing details. Fondant can be cut into designs, formed into shapes, flavored (white chocolate is popular), or tinted. Poured fondant is used to glaze petits fours and other tiny confections; it has a shiny finish and a sugary taste.

{ SPECIAL CONSIDERATIONS }

If chilled too long in the refrigerator, fondant may sweat when it is removed. If the cake will be displayed in a cool environment, the condensation will evaporate. If it will be displayed on a hot, humid day, avoid refrigerating but be sure to keep the cake in an air-conditioned room. Fondant actually helps keep cakes fresh, so it's often used for those too big to be refrigerated.

FRESH/CRYSTALLIZED FLOWERS

{ DESCRIPTION }

Fresh, in-season edible flowers offer an easy, inexpensive cake-decorating option. Crystallized flowers—which are coated with egg whites and then superfine sugar—are sturdier and longer-lasting.

{ SPECIAL CONSIDERATIONS }

Only edible and nontoxic inedible flowers (see "Using Edible Flowers," page 225) can touch the cake; remove nontoxic ones before serving. Toxic flowers should never be used. Flowers should be added at the last minute, so coordinate with your florist. To ensure crystallized flowers are safe for all of your guests, ask your baker to use meringue powder or powdered egg whites rather than liquid egg whites.

FRESH/SUGARED FRUIT

{ DESCRIPTION }

Dainty whole fruits, including lady apples, Seckel pears, plums, grapes, figs, berries, and cherries, make elegant and affordable decorations, either plain or sugared. Sliced citrus fruits can be candied in a simple syrup, which keeps them full of flavor and prevents their juices from discoloring the frosting. Fresh fruit purées can be mixed with buttercream or whipped cream as a topping or filling.

{ SPECIAL CONSIDERATIONS }

Whole (never sliced) fresh fruits should be added just before the cake is displayed. If they're placed too early, their juice can bleed into the frosting. To ensure sugared fruits are safe for all of your guests, ask your baker to use meringue powder or powdered egg whites rather than liquid egg whites.

GANACHE

{ DESCRIPTION }

This rich, velvety frosting is made from either white or dark chocolate and heavy cream. When poured over a cake, ganache is very shiny; cooled and spread, it has a rich, matte look. Ganache, which is sometimes whipped for a lighter texture, is also used as a filling or piped into decorations. White-chocolate ganache can be tinted.

{ SPECIAL CONSIDERATIONS }

Avoid pairing ganache with a light cake such as a delicate sponge or angel food; this thick frosting needs a cake it won't overpower, such as pound, chocolate, spice, or nut cakes. Keep in mind that ganache is sensitive to humidity.

GUM PASTE

{ DESCRIPTION }

Also called sugar paste, this elastic sugar dough can be tinted and then used to make delicate flower petals and other intricate shapes.

{ SPECIAL CONSIDERATIONS }

If fresh flowers or fruit won't be an option, realistic versions of your favorites can be rendered in sugar paste well ahead of time. And, if your cake will be displayed for a long period of time at the reception, these flowers won't wilt like fresh ones will.

MARZIPAN

{ DESCRIPTION }

An easy-to-tint paste made of ground almonds, sugar, and sometimes egg whites, marzipan is used to form edible cake decorations in such shapes as flowers or fruit. With its pronounced almond flavor, marzipan pairs well with citrus, apricot, raspberry, cherry, and bittersweet or semisweet chocolate. A thin layer of marzipan can also be used to cover a cake (similar to fondant) or as a filling.

{ SPECIAL CONSIDERATIONS }

For those wanting a seamless finish without having to use fondant, marzipan is a good (and more flavorful) alternative. Like fondant, marzipan helps keep a cake fresh when used as a covering.

MERINGUE (SWISS/ITALIAN)

{ DESCRIPTION }

Made from egg whites, sugar, and cream of tartar, meringue whips into a billowy icing. It can be spread over layers or piped into flowers or peaks for a voluptuous look. It is opaque enough, too, to cover any type of cake underneath. Meringue can also be piped into decorations and baked, which helps the meringue keep its shape and gives it crunch.

{ SPECIAL CONSIDERATIONS }

Meringue does not hold up well in humidity. If the cake has to be transported, it should be carefully packed, because meringue's soft texture is easily marred. Baked decorations are sturdier, but you may want to have your baker make extras in case of breakage. The egg whites are sufficiently heated so there are no health concerns.

PASTILLAGE

{ DESCRIPTION }

Pastillage is a pliable sugar dough that is most often used to create sculptural designs that are not meant to be eaten (such as a cake topper or other removable decoration, like the ones between the tiers of this wedding cake).

{ SPECIAL CONSIDERATIONS }

Pastillage is sturdier than gum paste and dries more quickly; it also holds up well in high humidity, but it is not as versatile as gum paste or rolled fondant. Once dried, pastillage decorations will shatter easily. If they will be added on-site, make sure your baker packages them carefully and makes plenty of extras to replace any that break.

ROYAL ICING

{ DESCRIPTION }

This decorative icing is made from confectioners' sugar and egg whites (or meringue powder). It can be thick enough to be piped or thinned for "flood work" (filling in designs). Since it hardens quickly, it is ideal for making detailed shapes ahead of time. It can also be piped directly onto cake tiers and works beautifully for delicate work, including dotted swiss and stringwork.

{ SPECIAL CONSIDERATIONS }

Details made from royal icing should be added on-site, as they're prone to snapping. Your cake maker will want to make extra for any last-minute touch-ups before the cake is displayed. To ensure the royal icing is safe for all of your guests, ask your baker to use meringue powder or powdered egg whites rather than liquid egg whites.

PRESENTING THE CAKE

With all the other details requiring your attention, it might be easy to overlook how your cake will be displayed. There are many unexpected ways to share your cake with your guests, and you should choose one that reflects your personality and the style of your cake and event.

- INDIVIDUAL CAKES, WHETHER CUPCAKES or more formally dressed little confections, are charming and special, as each guest has his or her own. You can stack cake stands to form a tower to mimic the tiers of a formal cake or create a buffet of little cakes. You can also have a small cake serve as the centerpiece for each table.

- DEPENDING ON THE SETTING, you might find wonderful alternatives to a standard cake table. If your reception will be held outdoors, stroll around the grounds ahead of time to see what you can find, such as a sturdy stone pedestal or an interesting sculptural table.

- IF YOU PLAN TO OFFER an array of sweets, you could present the cake on the dessert table. A grand, towering cake would appear even more impressive on a long table surrounded by other fancy delicacies; a simple cake could be accompanied by platters of cookies and other homespun treats.

- EVEN A STANDARD CAKE TABLE can be made to feel distinctive. Swaths of tulle look dreamy. A red checkered cloth is fitting for an informal gathering outdoors. A canopy made from a sheer fabric would frame the cake beautifully (and would also help protect it from sunlight at an outdoor wedding).

- A MANNER OF PRESENTATION can even influence the cake's style and design; for example, if you have a collection of vintage cake stands, you may want to have three or four smaller cakes instead of one.

{SWEET SETUP} *If you love desserts, don't stop with a cake: Indulge in a buffet of delights. For the most mouthwatering presentation, limit your color palette and set the table with both grand confections—like this towering chocolate-embellished Ron Ben-Israel cake—and bite-size goodies; guests will love sampling from the tempting display.*

FORMAL & FANCIFUL

GOLDEN
TRIMMINGS

{GOLDEN TRIMMINGS} *Three square cake tiers are embellished with a sparkling array of trims and ribbons. The cake board is just as ornate but is actually quite simple to create from one-inch-thick plywood painted pink and trimmed with ribbon. The legs are fashioned out of pink and gold beads.*

{LACE CANOPY} *A veil-like covering frames a fondant cake with gum-paste lace, by Ron Ben-Israel. He based the intricate pattern on a swatch of Chantilly lace.*

{DESSERT CART} *A vintage trolley suits the color and fiddlehead pattern of this cake. It also provides an ideal place for the necessary cake accoutrements: plates, forks, and napkins.*

{"GIFT" TABLE} *This trio of beautifully wrapped cakes is just the thing to offer guests at the end of the night. The crowning amaryllis "bows" are made from sugar paste by Ron Ben-Israel.*

DESSERT
CART

"GIFT"
TABLE

NAMESAKE
CAKE

RUSTIC & RELAXED

{NAMESAKE CAKE} *Festive fabric slung over branches creates a natural frame while protecting dessert from the sun. Decorated simply with buttercream, icing letters from the supermarket, and a topper, this cake is perfect for the playful display.*

{CUPCAKE TIERS} *Square stands tied with tailored ribbons are topped with cupcakes by Gail Watson; the graduated platforms echo the shape of a more traditional cake.*

{MINI CAKES} *Individual wedding cakes make everyone feel like the guest of honor. These tiny cakes are covered with rolled fondant and tiny blooms and berries.*

{CENTERPIECE CAKE} *This cake works double duty: it's both centerpiece and dessert. The confection, made by Perfect Endings of Napa, California, is crowned with handcrafted sugar clematis, dogwood, hydrangea, jasmine, and wild roses.*

CUPCAKE TIERS

MINI CAKES

CENTERPIECE CAKE

A CAKE'S ACCESSORIES

BRIDE AND GROOM CAKE TOPPERS

New versions are available, but vintage cake toppers offer a particularly charming finishing touch to a cake. You'll find them at flea markets and online auctions, often for less than $25. To determine their era, consider the material (plastic pieces were made in the second half of last century) and the style of the couple. The hairstyles of two of our brides (second row, left, and bottom row, center) indicate the couples may date to the 1920s. The bride in the red-dotted dress is probably from the '30s; the bride with the cropped red haircut (top row, center) was likely made in the '40s or '50s. Another indicator of age: Older ornaments tend to be a single piece, while newer ones have a separate bride and groom. Figures made in the likeness of older couples (bottom row, right) are meant to serve as reminders of the newlyweds' vow to grow old together. Some of these (top and bottom rows, right) are actually salt and pepper shakers, now collected as cake toppers.

CAKE BOARDS

Most wedding cakes are too large for a traditional footed cake stand. Instead, they are presented on a cake board, typically custom-cut from wood. To make one, start with a one- to two-inch-thick piece of plywood from the lumberyard cut to a diameter at least four inches larger than the bottom tier of the cake. You can sand, prime, and paint it, or coat it with icing: Spread the top of the board with thinned royal icing (add water until the icing smooths to a flat surface after five seconds) and allow it to harden for twenty-four hours. Secure ribbon with craft glue and add more trimmings if you wish.

PARTNERING WITH
A PROFESSIONAL

With so many ways to construct and design a cake and the myriad possible flavors and textures to choose from, working closely with an experienced baker is crucial to getting something that reflects your desires. Here are our guidelines for selecting the right baker for your celebration.

- FOR NAMES OF ESTABLISHED BAKERS, ask your other wedding vendors (the reception site manager and the caterer) as well as friends and relatives. You might also check with your favorite bakery for a recommendation.

- BEGIN BY CALLING AND ASKING SOME KEY QUESTIONS over the phone. The first one should be "Are you free on my wedding date?" If so, find out what kind of cakes he or she typically makes, what the price range is, and whether you can arrange an appointment for a tasting. All experienced bakers should have portfolios and offer cake tastings. Try to set one up for your first meeting.

- IDEALLY, THE BRIDE AND GROOM should meet with the baker together. If only one of you can go, it might help to bring a friend or relative for a second opinion.

- AS YOU LOOK THROUGH THE BAKER'S PORTFOLIO, you'll get an idea of whether your tastes and sensibilities mesh. Though most bakers will try to match your desires, a portfolio highlights a person's strengths. Be wary of bakers who promise to do anything you want, especially if you don't see anything similar in the portfolio. Experienced bakers will be able to tell you if your vision is realistic and, if not, suggest viable alternatives.

- DURING YOUR MEETING, EXPLAIN WHERE THE WEDDING IS BEING HELD, how many people will attend, and the time of the reception. A smart baker will ask you some of the following questions: What are the colors for your wedding? Is there a theme? Do you want a stacked cake or a pillared cake? What does your dress look like? Your answers will allow him or her to make appropriate suggestions.

- THE BAKER WILL MAKE SUGGESTIONS that suit the time and season. If you're planning an afternoon garden wedding in June, you might want something delicate, such as an almond pound cake filled with a light, creamy lemon curd blended with fresh blueberries and raspberries.

- DISCUSS HOW YOU WANT THE CAKE to be presented and served. Some couples prefer to have the cake displayed during the entire meal, others to have the cake revealed afterward. This is important when determining the type of filling and frosting, since some components hold up better over longer periods of time (out of refrigeration). It might also help you decide whether to have one cake for display and another for cutting in the kitchen and serving.

- BE SURE TO LET THE BAKER KNOW if you want to save the top tier for freezing, as this may affect how large a cake you will need. Some couples ask their bakers to make a small version of the cake to be enjoyed later.

- BUDGET, OF COURSE, WILL ALSO DICTATE which cake you choose. Discuss costs. Don't be afraid to say what your budget is. Your baker should give you suggestions that work with your numbers.

THE OFFICIAL AGREEMENT

Once you've decided on the cake, the baker will draw up a contract, which should detail everything you have discussed, including the exact design elements (some bakers provide a sketch of the cake), the cost per person, the delivery time, explicit directions to the reception site, and all necessary contact numbers. Before signing, carefully review the contract to ensure it doesn't have any hidden charges. For example, if the delivery exceeds the baker's ten-mile radius, a per-mile charge might be tacked on. (You should also find out if your caterer or the banquet hall charges a fee for cutting a cake that is brought in from outside.) The contract should also stipulate whether the baker or the florist will order the flowers, and who will decorate the cake with them. Upon signing the agreement, some bakers require that a 50 percent deposit be paid. Be sure to find out what portion of this is refundable, and under what conditions.

Many professional cake decorators do not refund any of the deposit once the contract has been signed, and for good reason: Once you have agreed to use their services, they may not be able to accept other clients for that day. So if for whatever reason you decide to cancel, they may not be able to replace your job with another. The secured deposit is your commitment to the baker, who in turn commits to having the agreed-upon cake on the designated day.

WHAT TO BUDGET FOR

- CAKES ARE USUALLY PRICED on a per-person, or per-slice, basis. Prices range from just a few dollars to as much as fifteen dollars, which means that a cake for one hundred guests could cost as little as a few hundred dollars or more than a thousand.

- WHERE IT COMES FROM will influence how the cake is priced. A simple cake made by a local bakery will be relatively inexpensive; a caterer or a specialty bakery may make a distinctive cake but will also charge more; and experienced cake designers, who are capable of making the most elaborate creations, are at the top end of the price range.

- THE COMPLEXITY OF THE DESIGN, the size of the cake, and the types and numbers of the fillings and frostings all add up to increase the cost. Labor-intensive handmade flourishes, such as chocolate roses or crystallized flowers, may be billed individually.

- LOCATION WILL DEFINITELY INFLUENCE the cost of the cake. In urban areas, such as New York City, San Francisco, and Chicago, you can expect to pay more than in some parts of the country.

WAYS TO SAVE

- INSTEAD OF ONE TOWERING CONFECTION, you could have a cake with fewer tiers for display and then have additional cakes that are cut in the kitchen for serving. These side cakes are easier (and less costly) for bakers to make than assembled tiers; because they can be plated ahead of time and served as soon as the couple cuts the cake, side cakes are also often preferred by caterers. This is especially helpful if you decide to add a sauce to the plates.

- IF YOU WANT A MULTI-TIERED CAKE but have a relatively small guest list (and need fewer slices), ask your baker to add tiers made of Styrofoam; they can be iced to match the others, and no one will ever know they're not edible. Or use long dowels to separate the tiers, and then conceal the dowels with flowers or other embellishments. This way, even a three-tier cake can have an impressive height.

- ORDER A MODERATELY PRICED, simply decorated cake, and make the focal point the cake topper. Vintage bride-and-groom figurines, wedding bells, horseshoes, a basket filled with fruit, or a pair of doves are classic symbols that can make a cake memorable. You can also use a miniature version of the bridal bouquet as the topper.

- IF USING FRESH FRUITS AND FLOWERS, make sure they're in season and available locally.

- DISPENSE WITH A DESSERT COURSE, and instead present the wedding cake with coffee and tea at the end of the meal.

TRADITIONS

- AT BRITISH WEDDINGS, the guests may be given boxes containing tiny slices of the cake—traditionally a lush fruitcake wrapped with marzipan and decorated with royal icing.

- THE FRENCH have their *pièce montée,* often a croquembouche, a tower of choux pastry puffs filled with pastry cream and dipped in caramel syrup.

- IN DENMARK, the weddings are celebrated with *kransekage,* a dainty-looking but remarkably dense eighteen-layer construction of almond-meringue rings.

- BEFORE A GREEK WEDDING, the women in the village gather together to bake wedding breads made from a sourdough starter and decorated with flower blossoms and beads.

- IN JAMAICA, the preparation of the wedding cake often begins when the engagement is announced. Raisins, prunes, mixed peels, and other dried fruits are soaked in white rum and wine. About two weeks before the wedding, the plumped fruits are used to make a heady black cake.

- IN BERMUDA, a multilayered fruitcake may be topped by a small cedar tree. The tree is planted after the ceremony and is expected to grow with the love of the couple.

- IN THE CONFARREATIO, the most prestigious and insoluble form of marriage in ancient Rome, the couple alone shared a sweet cake and ate it during the ceremony itself, not afterward.

GROOM'S CAKE

- ALTHOUGH ITS ROOTS stretch back to the Victorian era, the groom's cake is a tradition that has been eagerly adopted by many modern brides, particularly in the South, as a way to showcase the groom's interests or to simply add another flavor or a touch of whimsy to the dessert table.

- IT MAY BE SECONDARY, but the groom's cake is usually attention-getting, because novel and light-hearted adornments are popular. Many couples decorate this cake with an homage to the groom's heritage or to his favorite hobby or sport or team.

- THE GROOM'S CAKE CAN BE SERVED with the wedding cake, though some couples debut it early, serving it at the rehearsal dinner. And sometimes the old tradition is followed, and it is sliced and boxed for guests to take home as a favor.

- ACCORDING TO LEGEND, when an unmarried woman sleeps with a slice of groom's cake under her pillow, she will dream of her future husband.

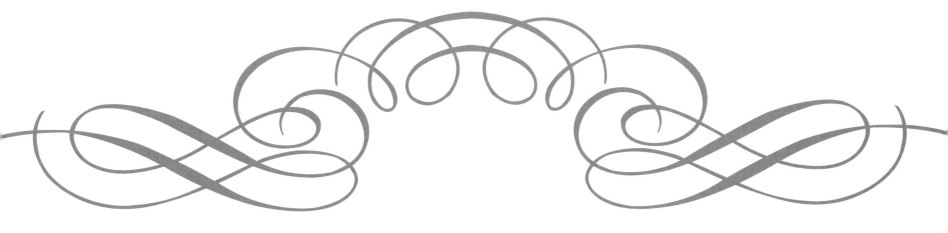

album of cakes

{EMBROIDERY CAKE} *The gum-paste flowers and royal-icing*
beading on this cake evoke classic white-on-white embroidery.
The ornate monogram was copied from one on the table runner.

No. 1
LEMON GROVE
CAKE

No. 2
DAISY GARDEN
CAKE

{NO. 1} *This cake's romantic leaf motif, rendered in royal icing, recalls a lush lemon grove. Strings of piped dots, mirrored by the stand's beaded edge, delineate tiers covered in imperial yellow fondant. The delicate lattice pattern repeats on the jacquard ribbon.* {NO. 2} *This winsome cake, complete with a canopy, is fitting for a garden wedding or a spring or summer day. The petals of tiny daisies are shaped with a balling tool; centers are royal icing coated with crystallized sugar. While still pliable, the fondant is imprinted with a dressmaker's wheel.*

{NO. 3} *The designs on this dramatic tower mimic the elaborate cake-decorating style of Joseph Lambeth, a master baker in England during the 1920s and '30s whose work Martha and Wendy both admire. Fine garlands and latticework are piped onto the fondant in royal icing, as are delicate roses and bunches of grapes. A satin-and-lace ribbon visually anchors the cake to its simple stand. For piping how-tos, see page 222. After several hours of decorating, the finishing touches are applied by Martha and Wendy with big smiles.*

No. 4
PINK LUSTERWARE CAKE

The sweet, shimmering details of nineteenth-century lusterware china inspired the borders on this cake. The motifs adorning each tier replicate patterns on actual china pieces. They were painted by (steady) hand onto the fondant-covered tiers using powdered food-coloring mixed with pure lemon extract. Plans for a teacup cake topper shown in the original sketch were discarded in favor of a cluster of peonies, since these flowers were a common element in lusterware patterns.

— SINGLE BAND

AT BASE OF TIER
LIKE RIBBON.

tea cup cake top

base?

Tru-Colour ROSE-RED

is a lovely color . . . and "lovely" is just the word that describes it. It's a color to which people react favorably. For instance, it is "so lovely a color" . . . that the other day when a piece was lying on the table . . . every one that came in reach ed over and picked it up. Print yo booklet Cover on Tru-Col RED and see how pl with th

The o

P

TILES
213 Cong

Mr. Ashley Hunter

No. 5

CREAMWARE CAKE

No. 6

BAHAMA ORCHID
CAKE

{NO. 5} *The reticulated pattern of eighteenth-century creamware china is mimicked on this multitiered cake.*
It was created with rolled fondant and the kind of cutters usually used for aspic and eyelet. Making the hundreds of decorative
holes is time-consuming, and you'll need to work quickly so the fondant doesn't dry out. Sugar paste was used for the
"embroidered" flowers on the top and base. {NO. 6} *The edges of square tiers are softened with buttercream beading and a*
few prettily placed cattleya orchids. Cake by Todd Johnson for Dune at One & Only Ocean Club, Bahamas.

{NO. 7} *Graceful lettering adorns the icing on a geometric cake; placed end to end, the arcs and swirls almost seem more like a dreamy pattern than like initials. See page 217 for the how-to.* {NO. 8} *A few extraordinary roses fashioned to look like fabric flowers add a touch of couture to a cake by Ron Ben-Israel based on the quilted fabric known as* matelassé. *The leaves on the cake (fondant formed in a silicone mold) contrast with the textured bands (made by pressing fondant onto a grid) wrapping the tiers. The cake board is covered with fondant and edged in a vintage silk ribbon.*

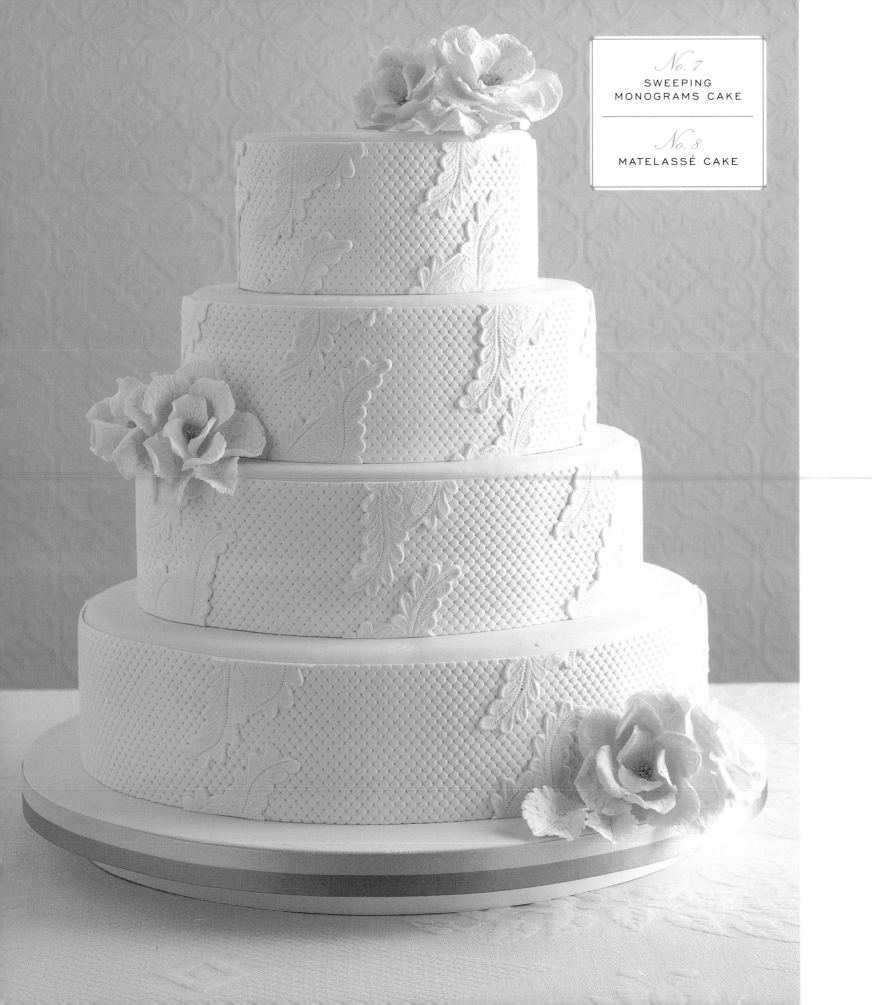

No. 9
BUTTONED-UP
CAKE

{NO. 9} *Buttons in playful patterns transform a traditional fondant-covered cake into an altogether stylish one; they are made from gum paste and tinted ivory. More buttons top petit-four favors, set on candy wrappers and tucked into glassine-lined boxes. These black and white boxes have their lids swapped. Cake and favors by Gail Watson.*

SEVEN-TIER COCONUT CAKE
SERVES 360

To give this impressive cake even more height, we set it atop
a double-thick wooden cake board.

*2 each 6-, 8-, 10-, 12-, 14-, 16-, and 18-inch
round layers of Coconut Cake (recipe follows)*

7 pieces corresponding-size ³⁄₁₆-inch-thick foam board

4 batches Coconut Buttercream (page 238)

4 batches Swiss Meringue Buttercream (page 238)

54 wooden dowels (¼ inch in diameter, 4⅛ inches long)

1 pound crystallized coconut

1 pound unsweetened coconut chips

1 pound shredded unsweetened coconut

1 cake mat (8 inches; optional)

1 round wooden cake platform (20-inch diameter)

12 batches Coconut Crème Anglaise, for serving (recipe follows)

1. Prepare the tiers: Trim and split the layers. On corresponding-size foam boards, fill each set of layers with coconut buttercream to create 4-inch-tall tiers. Thinly coat the tiers with plain Swiss meringue buttercream to seal in the crumbs. Chill until set, about 30 minutes. Frost the tiers with more Swiss meringue buttercream.

2. Reinforce the tiers: Insert 16 dowels vertically into the 18-inch tier, making a circle with 12 dowels about 2 inches from the edge and placing 4 in a square in the center. Insert 10 dowels each into both the 16- and 14-inch tiers, placing 1 in the center and 9 in a circle 2 inches from the edge. In the same manner, insert 8 dowels into the 12-inch tier and 6 into the 10-inch tier. Insert 4 dowels into the 8-inch tier in a square about 3 inches from the edge.

3. Decorate the tiers: Press the crystallized coconut, coconut chips, and shredded coconut onto the tiers to completely cover the buttercream.

4. Assemble the tiers: Place the cake mat or several drops of hot glue on the cake platform; center and place the 18-inch tier on top. Carefully center and stack the remaining tiers in descending order.

5. To serve, spoon coconut crème anglaise onto each plate; top with a slice of cake.

"For one of my significant birthdays, my daughter, Alexis, created a giant coconut cake frosted in white buttercream and enhanced with hand-shaved fresh coconut. It was such a spectacular success, we've since suggested tiered coconut cakes, like the one shown here, for weddings."

Martha

{NO. 10} *This majestic cake gives coconut lovers several reasons to rejoice: the seven tiers of coconut cake are filled with coconut buttercream and decorated with Swiss meringue butter-cream, candied coconut, and two different types of coconut flakes. The different-size flakes cling easily to the buttercream when pressed.*

COCONUT CAKE

MAKES 16 CUPS BATTER

For approximate batter amounts and baking times,
see note below. Make the batter in separate batches.

1 pound (4 sticks) unsalted butter,
at room temperature, plus more for the pans

7¼ cups cake flour (not self-rising), sifted,
plus more for the pans

2 tablespoons plus 1 teaspoon baking powder

1 teaspoon salt

2 cups canned unsweetened coconut milk

6 tablespoons milk

4 cups sugar

1 tablespoon plus 1 teaspoon pure vanilla extract

16 large egg whites, at room temperature

1. Preheat the oven to 375°F. Brush the cake pans with butter. Line each with parchment paper; butter again, and dust with flour, tapping out any excess. Set aside.

2. Sift together the flour, baking powder, and salt into a large bowl; set aside. Stir the milks together; set aside. Put the butter and all but 2 tablespoons of the sugar in the bowl of an electric mixer fitted with the paddle attachment; cream on medium speed until pale and fluffy, about 5 minutes. Beat in the vanilla.

3. With the mixer on low speed, add the flour mixture in four batches, alternating with the milk mixture and beginning and ending with flour. Mix until combined, scraping down the sides of the bowl as needed. Set aside.

4. Switch to a whisk attachment; beat the egg whites in a clean bowl until soft peaks form. With the mixer on medium-high speed, gradually add the remaining 2 tablespoons sugar. Beat on high speed until the peaks are stiff and glossy, about 30 seconds.

5. Gently fold the egg whites into the batter with a rubber spatula. Divide among the prepared pans. Smooth the tops with an offset spatula. Firmly tap the pans on a work surface to release any air bubbles.

6. Bake until a cake tester inserted into the centers comes out clean and the cakes are golden and firm to the touch. Let cool completely in the pans on wire racks before unmolding. Refrigerate, wrapped well in plastic wrap, until ready to assemble the cake, up to 3 days, or freeze for 1 month.

Approximate batter amounts and baking times for 2-inch-deep round pans: 6-inch: 2½ cups, 35 minutes; 8-inch: 3 cups, 40 minutes; 10-inch: 6 cups, 50 minutes; 12-inch: 8 cups, 55 minutes; 14-inch: 15 cups, 1 hour; 16-inch: 22 cups, 1 hour 10 minutes; 18-inch: 24 cups, 1 hour 15 minutes

COCONUT CRÈME ANGLAISE

MAKES ABOUT 4 CUPS

You will need twelve batches to serve with the cake; this recipe can be multiplied. Crème anglaise can be refrigerated in an airtight container for up to three days. Before serving, whisk until smooth.

4 large eggs, at room temperature

½ cup sugar

Pinch of salt

3½ cups canned unsweetened coconut milk

1 cup heavy cream

1. Prepare an ice-water bath; set aside. Put the eggs, sugar, and salt in the bowl of an electric mixer fitted with the whisk attachment; beat on medium-high speed until pale and thick, 3 to 4 minutes. Meanwhile, bring the coconut milk and cream to a boil in a medium saucepan; remove from the heat.

2. With the mixer on low speed, gradually pour half of the hot milk mixture into the egg mixture. Return the mixture to the pan. Cook over medium-low heat, stirring constantly with a wooden spoon, until the mixture is thick enough to coat the back of the spoon and hold a line drawn by your finger, about 5 minutes. Pass the mixture through a fine sieve into a medium bowl. Place the bowl in the ice-water bath; stir the crème anglaise occasionally until chilled.

No. 11
CHERRY
CHEESECAKE

No. 12
ROSE BASKET CAKE

{NO. 11} *Bands of white chocolate wrap a creamy cheesecake. White cherries such as Rainier or Queen Anne are dipped in egg white and then superfine sugar and used to fill the "moats" created by the bands. The cherry stems, twisting naturally, soften the lines of this geometric creation.* {NO. 12} *In a lush and luscious cake, roses are arranged between buttercream tiers piped in a basket-weave pattern to resemble wicker. Atop the cake, a ceramic pot (with no hole in the bottom) is overflowing with roses anchored in floral foam; to support the weight of the pot, insert dowels into the top tier.*

Charlotte aux Fruits Rouges

{NO.13} *In this charlotte, by Florian Bellanger, ladyfingers surround a filling of raspberry mousse, raspberries, and fraises des bois, or wild strawberries, on soft almond biscuits. Ribbon is wrapped around each tier.*

{NO.14} *A shower of red rose petals floats down over the tiers of a pristine white cake by Susan Spungen. Tiny beads are piped at the base of each tier.*

No. 13
LADYFINGER
CHARLOTTE CAKE

No. 14
DRIFTING PETALS
CAKE

No. 15
PINK MACAROON
CAKE

No. 16
PRETTY PIPED
BOWS CAKE

{NO. 15} *A majestic design turns a bit coquettish when it's festooned with macaroons—the quintessential
French treats—and dressed up in flirty pink. Rubber stamps were used to imprint the fondant with its graphic pattern.
At the top, a single macaroon rests in a miniature compote.* {NO. 16} *The bows that adorn this cake
are made up of royal-icing loops—approximately 1,000 of them!—each one piped separately then allowed to dry before
being inserted into dollops of royal icing; Swiss dots complete the base.*

{NO. 17} *This tower of truffles is inspired by the croquembouche, the traditional French wedding cake. We made 300 truffles for this, rolled them in different-colored cocoa powders, and cut them in half. Beneath them are layers of yellow butter cake filled and frosted with a dark ganache.*

{NO. 18} *The honeycomb pattern on this fanciful, fondant-covered cake was imprinted with a rubber stamp. Pinpricked trails evoke the meandering flight of papier-mâché bumblebees. A hive made of strips of quilling paper crowns the lemon-and-honey-infused confection. The beveled edges on these tiers were hand-cut, but beveled cake pans can be purchased.*

No. 17
TOWER OF
TRUFFLES CAKE

No. 18
BEEHIVE CAKE

No. 19

APPLESAUCE
CAKE

No. 20

IRONSTONE
CAKE

{NO. 19} *Caramel-dipped lady and crab apples glisten atop a moist, spiced applesauce cake with cream cheese filling.*
The top tier is supported with walnut dowels; apple-tree branches and leaves fill the space between the tiers.
{NO. 20} *Its subtle aesthetic made the sturdy dinnerware known as English ironstone popular in the nineteenth century.*
This fondant-covered confection takes on the quietly raised pattern and charm of the original.

CITRUS CELEBRATION CAKE
SERVES 90

If your refrigerator is not large enough to hold the assembled cake, decorate the tiers separately and refrigerate. At the reception site, stack them before adding the orange slices in step 5. The orange slices can be placed on the cake up to six hours before serving.

2 each 6-, 9-, and 12-inch-round layers of
Moist Yellow Cake (recipe follows)

3 pieces corresponding-size ³⁄₁₆-inch-thick foam board

2 batches Vanilla-Bean Buttercream (recipe follows)

1 batch Lemon Simple Syrup (recipe follows)

2 batches Lemon Curd (recipe follows)

1 cake mat (8-inch square; optional)

1 cake platter (20-inch diameter)

14 wooden dowels (¼ inch in diameter, 4⅛ inches long)

3 to 4 batches Candied Orange Slices (recipe follows)

Variety of small citrus fruits and leaves, rinsed well

36 gum-paste orange blossoms (see Sources, page 254)

1. Prepare the tiers: Trim and split the 12-inch cake layers. Set one bottom piece on a 12-inch-diameter foam board, securing with a dollop of buttercream, and place the foam board on a cake turntable. Turn the other bottom section upside down (do not stack layers yet); this will be the top of the tier. Brush the top and sides of each section with lemon simple syrup. Using a pastry bag fitted with a plastic coupler, pipe a dam of buttercream around all sections except the top one. Fill the centers inside the dams with 1½ cups lemon curd each. Stack the sections, pressing each gently to adhere. On the turntable, adjust the tier to be level, and then coat it with a thin layer of icing to seal in crumbs. Refrigerate. Similarly trim, fill, and crumb-coat on foam board the 9-inch tier with 1 cup curd per layer, and the 6-inch tier with ¾ cup curd per layer.

2. Frost the tiers: Remove one tier from the refrigerator. Place on the turntable, and coat smoothly with buttercream. Return to the refrigerator for at least 30 minutes. Repeat with the remaining tiers. *(continued on page 74)*

"Lemon anything has always been my favorite flavor for dessert. This glorious yellow confection, its layers brushed with lemon syrup and filled with lemon curd, makes a fresh-tasting and glistening tiered cake."

Martha

{NO. 21} *This cake's tiers are iced with buttercream, piped with lines and dots, and encircled by candied navel orange slices. The shapes of the tiers are softened by baby mandarins, kumquats, and clementines on their branches, along with sugar-paste orange blossoms. Vanilla bean in the butter-cream adds tiny flecks and a heavenly perfume and flavor.*

3. Assemble and decorate the tiers: Place the cake mat or several drops of hot glue in the center of the platter. Place the 12-inch tier on the mat. Insert 8 dowels in a circle 3 inches from the edge of the tier; set the platter on the turntable. Using a round (Ateco #6) tip, and beginning at the back of the tier, pipe buttercream in a vertical line from the top edge to the bottom. Pipe vertical lines all around the tier, spacing them ¼ inch apart. Use the same tip to pipe dots around the top and bottom edges. If the buttercream begins to soften, empty the bag into the bowl of buttercream, and stir; refill the bag halfway. Once the 12-inch tier is decorated, place the 9-inch tier on top and insert 6 dowels in a circle 2½ inches from the edge. Decorate as before, then stack the 6-inch tier on top, and decorate it. Place the decorated cake in the refrigerator.

4. Attach the candied orange slices: Drain the orange slices in a single layer on a wire rack, about 20 minutes. Cut each slice in half; lay on damp paper towels. Place the cake on the turntable; starting from the back, attach slices to the side of each tier, aligning the cut edges with the top. Trim ½ inch from the cut edge of the remaining slices. Position the trimmed slices on the tops of the tiers, so they meet with the top edges of the placed slices in an alternating pattern. Pipe buttercream dots on the oranges at the rims of the tiers, as shown.

5. To serve, place the cake on a serving table and, using citrus fruits and leaves, decorate the base and top of the cake. Place gum-paste orange blossoms among the citrus and leaves.

YELLOW CAKE
MAKES 11 CUPS BATTER

For approximate batter amounts and baking times, see note below; you will need to make enough batter to fill each cake pan three-quarters full (a total of about 25½ cups). The batter can be made in separate batches for the larger cake layers.

*12 ounces (3 sticks) unsalted butter,
at room temperature, plus more for pans*

*4 cups cake flour (not self-rising), sifted,
plus more for pans*

1 tablespoon baking powder

3 cups sugar

6 large eggs, separated, at room temperature

1½ cups milk

½ teaspoon salt

---

1. Preheat the oven to 325°F. Butter the cake pans and line each with a parchment-paper circle cut to size. Butter and flour the parchment; set the pans aside. Sift together the flour and baking powder three times; set aside.

2. In the bowl of an electric mixer fitted with the paddle attachment, cream the butter and sugar together until fluffy. Add egg yolks one at a time, beating until incorporated after each. Add the flour mixture to the egg mixture in three additions alternately with milk, starting and ending with flour.

3. In the clean bowl of an electric mixer fitted with the whisk attachment, beat the egg whites with the salt until stiff but not dry. Mix a quarter of the whites into the batter, and then fold in the remaining whites.

4. Pour the batter into the pans. Bake until the tops are golden brown and a tester inserted into the centers comes out clean. Cool the cakes in the pans for 20 minutes. Run a knife around the outside of the cakes. Turn out the cakes onto wire racks, remove the papers, and reinvert the cakes to cool, top side up. Wrap the cooled cakes in plastic; refrigerate at least overnight before using. The cakes will keep, refrigerated, for 2 days, or for 3 months frozen.

Approximate batter amounts and baking times for 3-inch-deep round pans: 6-inch: 3½ cups, 1 hour; 9-inch: 7 cups, 1 hour 10 minutes; 12-inch: 15 cups, 1 hour 35 minutes

VANILLA-BEAN BUTTERCREAM
MAKES 7 CUPS

*2 pounds (8 sticks) unsalted butter,
at room temperature*

2½ cups sugar

10 large egg whites

1½ vanilla beans, split and scraped

1 tablespoon pure vanilla extract

1. In the bowl of an electric mixer fitted with the paddle attachment, beat the butter until fluffy and pale. Set aside.

2. Combine the sugar and egg whites in a clean, heat-proof mixer bowl; place the bowl over a pan of simmering water. Whisk until the sugar dissolves and the whites are warm to the touch, 3 to 4 minutes.

3. Transfer the bowl to the mixer; with the whisk attachment beat on medium-high until fluffy and cool, and stiff peaks form, about 10 minutes. Reduce the speed to medium-low; add the beaten butter a few tablespoons at a time, beating well after each addition. Add the vanilla bean scrapings and extract.

4. Switch to the paddle; beat on the lowest speed to remove air bubbles, 3 to 5 minutes. Buttercream can be stored in an airtight container in the refrigerator for up to 3 days. Bring to room temperature and beat until smooth before using.

LEMON SIMPLE SYRUP
MAKES 3½ CUPS

3 cups sugar

*½ cup freshly squeezed lemon juice
(about 4 lemons)*

In a 2-quart saucepan, bring the sugar and 1½ cups water to a boil. Reduce the heat; simmer for 3 minutes. Let cool completely. Stir in the lemon juice. Refrigerate in an airtight container for up to 1 week.

LEMON CURD
MAKES ABOUT 7 CUPS

*Grated zest of 7 lemons (about 6 tablespoons),
plus 1¾ cups freshly squeezed lemon juice
(about 13 lemons total)*

10 large whole eggs

5 large egg yolks

1¾ cups sugar

*1¾ cups (3½ sticks) cold unsalted butter,
cut into pieces*

1. Whisk together the lemon zest and juice, whole eggs, egg yolks, and sugar in a large, heavy saucepan. Cook over medium heat, stirring constantly with a wooden spoon, until the mixture thickens, 20 to 25 minutes.

2. Remove from the heat, and stir in the butter, one piece at a time, until melted. Strain the mixture through a fine-mesh sieve into a medium bowl. Cover with plastic wrap, pressing it directly on the surface. Refrigerate until chilled, up to 3 days.

CANDIED ORANGE SLICES
MAKES 2 TO 3 DOZEN

You will need eighty slices for the Citrus Celebration Cake tiers. The slices can be stored in an airtight container in the refrigerator for up to one week.

4 small to medium navel oranges

2 cups sugar

1. Wash the oranges, trim the tops and bottoms, and cut into ⅛-inch-thick slices (7 to 9 slices per orange). Remove any seeds.

2. In a large saucepan over medium heat, combine the sugar with 2 cups water. Bring to a boil, and simmer until clear, about 5 minutes. Add enough slices to fit in one layer; simmer, turning occasionally, for 20 to 40 minutes, or until translucent yet still orange. Transfer the slices to a heat-proof container. Repeat with the remaining slices. Pour the syrup into the container with the slices; let cool before using or storing.

{NO. 22} *Daisy clusters are tucked into grosgrain ribbon "hat" bands. Each gum-paste flower is created petal by petal and allowed to dry for twenty-four hours before being assembled. The leaves are fashioned from gum paste in three shades of green and coated in sugar. The fondant for the tiers was rolled out on straw matting to create texture.*

{NO. 23} *The edible pleats here recall the crinolines beneath a cream puff of a wedding dress. White wafer papers, cut with scallop scissors and folded, were painted with gold luster dust and petal dust in pinks and greens. (Painting them before folding makes the job go more quickly.) They were then piped with white royal icing and attached to the mint-green fondant-covered tiers with more royal icing.*

No. 24
PEARL AND SHELL
CAKE

No. 25
PRIMROSE
CAKE

{NO. 24} *In this cake by Gail Watson, confectionary pearls of graduating sizes and scallop shells formed from gum paste are brushed with luster dust for opalescence. Impressions in the ivory fondant were made with an embossing tool. Sugar sprinkled on the tops of the tiers and the cake board sparkles like white sand.* {NO. 25} *This four-tiered cake's gum-paste flowers and leaves appear to support the weight of the tiers but actually hide the dowels that do the work. The primulas may be made in advance, but the leaves need to be applied to the tiers when they are fresh and still pliable.*

Octagon Pastel Boxes

PANTONE® 9320 C	strawberry
PANTONE® 9561 C	mint
PANTONE® 9443 C	
PANTONE® 9203 C	espresso
slue	
PANTONE® 9362 C	blackberry
slue	

...agon, each tier has a tapered layer...
...scent pastel (see swatc...
...Matching dotte...
...und 4 s...
...n non-...

FRENCH CONFECTIONARY BOX CAKE

All tied up and ready to go, this lovely cake was influenced by boxes found in Ladurée, a Parisian tea salon and pastry shop. We tweaked their shape slightly and tried to match the pastel hues with color chips to use as a guide in tinting the fondant that covers the tiers. The box lids are the actual cake; the bottoms, also wrapped in fondant, are cake risers. The gold bands were painted on. To achieve a straight line, place a tier on a turntable; position the head of a thin brush on the tier and rotate the turntable, keeping the brush in place. Golden dots of royal icing edge each band. The whole package is tied together, just like the original inspiration, with a taffeta ribbon.

{NO. 27} *Techniques used by dressmakers to turn fabric into flowers inspired this cake. A combination of fondant and white chocolate envelops the cake and serves as a pristine background for the gum-paste "appliqués." Buttercream dots frame the designs.* {NO. 28} *Cupcakes are crowned with fondant hearts cut with a cookie cutter and imprinted with the bride's and groom's first initials using a rubber stamp. Those bearing a B are paired with napkins marked with an H, and vice versa. The cake tiers are made of Styrofoam and boards, with three-inch-wide doily trim.*

No. 27
APPLIQUÉ CAKE

No. 28
HOMESPUN
CUPCAKE TOWER

84

{NO. 29} *A delicious reinterpretation of a Corinthian column, this cake by Claire Perez is unusually grand.*
The column's fluting is created by carefully pressing an offset spatula into the fondant. Acanthus leaves made of fondant bring
an organic touch to the gently graduated tiers. {NO. 30} *Flecks of vanilla bean in buttercream icing give this cake*
the appearance of an enchanting harbinger of spring: a delicate robin's egg. The cloudlike zigzag flourishes were piped with
a large petal tip. Alongside, white dragées are joined with royal icing and tied with thin gold cord.

{NO. 31} *In a grand tower of a cake, five deep hexagonal tiers are piped with buttercream in opposite directions using a star tip for a patchwork effect. The initials are made of air-dried meringue. Extra meringue letters were made, so each slice could be served with its own R. Here's a great tip: You don't necessarily need specialty pans for an unusually shaped cake. For example, you can cut hexagons from standard round tiers.*

{NO. 32} *A graphic embellishment is all the more striking against rich, chocolate-brown fondant. These royal-icing designs, piped in white and light-brown dots, echo the petal shape of the cake tiers and stand. A pattern was first pinpricked into the fondant and then piped over. The cascading design on the top tier forms an intricate, many-petaled flower.*
{NO. 33} *Stems, berries, and flowers in the style of crewelwork edge their way over the tiers of this striking cake by Ron Ben-Israel. The raised "yarn" of white sugar paste is emphasized by the smoothness of the café-au-lait-colored fondant. The wooden cake boards are trimmed with grosgrain ribbons with white detailing on the edges.*

No. 32
DOTTED PETALS
CAKE

No. 33
CREWELWORK CAKE

{NO. 34} *Simple designs, like the luscious buttercream blooms atop these tiny cakes, can make a big impression. Just three inches high, these beauties could be the highlight of a dessert buffet or be served at each place. If you're making (or ordering) small cakes, keep in mind that they are often more time-consuming (and thus more expensive) than a single larger cake.*

{NO. 35} *Hundreds of tightly curled, tempered-white-chocolate straws encircle a trio of cake layers, which are topped with golden raspberries. The raspberries get a sifting of powdered sugar.*

{NO. 36} *Covered with Swiss meringue buttercream and garnished with Champagne grapes and Seckel pears,*
this cake has a rustic elegance. A cake stand of stoneware is supported by dowels inside the bottom tier. {NO. 37} *The green*
fondant exterior of this elegant cake, by Wendy and Bill Yosses, is trimmed in stripes of cocoa-colored satin ribbon.
The textured "foliage" was made by painting melted chocolate onto real mint leaves, and then peeling away the mint when
the chocolate hardened. (See page 230 for how to make chocolate leaves.)

No. 36
TUSCAN GRAPES
CAKE

No. 37
CHOCOLATE
MINT CAKE

Woodland Nut Cake
for 250

WOODLAND NUT CAKE

SERVES 250

Royal-icing dots are piped along the crimped border on each tier.
The cake would be just as lovely without the dots.

*3 each 7¾ by 5⅝-inch, 10¾ by 7⅝-inch, 13 by 9⅞-inch,
and 16½ by 12⅜-inch oval layers of Almond-Hazelnut Cake (recipe follows)*

4 pieces corresponding-size 3⁄16-inch-thick foam board

4 batches Pistachio Buttercream (recipe follows)

6 batches Marzipan, 1 batch reserved for making nuts and leaves (page 243)

1 oval cake platter or board (20 by 15½ inches)

28 wooden dowels (¼ inch in diameter, 6 inches long)

Petal dust food coloring (such as Moss Green)

1. Prepare the tiers: Trim the layers. On corresponding-size foam boards, fill the layers with buttercream. Thinly coat with buttercream to seal in the crumbs. Refrigerate for at least 1 hour.

2. Cover the tiers: Between two pieces of plastic, roll marzipan into a 25 x 30-inch oval. Center, drape, and smooth the marzipan over the largest tier. Cut the excess at the bottom with a pizza wheel. While the marzipan is still soft, use a fluted pastry wheel to crimp a decorative edge around the top of the cake. Repeat, covering the remaining tiers.

3. Assemble the tiers, flush at the back: Center and place the largest tier on the cake platter. Insert 12 dowels, 10 in an oval and 2 evenly off-center. Dab the top with a little buttercream. Place the 13-inch tier on top. Insert 10 dowels, 8 in an oval and 2 off-center. Dab the top with buttercream. Place the 10¾-inch tier on top. Insert the remaining 6 dowels in an oval. Dab the top with buttercream. Center and place the 7¾-inch tier on top.

4. Decorate the tiers: With a fine paintbrush, dust the crimped border with the moss-green petal dust. Decorate the tiers and top of the cake with marzipan nuts and leaves.

Approximate marzipan amounts (13 pounds total): 7¾-inch tier, 2 pounds; 10¾-inch tier, 2½ pounds; 13-inch tier, 3½ pounds; 16½-inch tier, 5 pounds

"The moist, dense almond-hazelnut cake layers are sealed in marzipan, making this cake perfect for a large wedding—it will hold up well and slice very neatly."

Martha

{NO. 38} *Pistachios, almonds, and filberts as they appear in their pods, as well as almonds and pecans in the shell, are all crafted out of marzipan. "Ledges" for the embellishments are created by setting the tiers flush in the back. The interior pairs almond-hazelnut layers and pale-green pistachio buttercream filling.*

ALMOND-HAZELNUT CAKE
MAKES 6 CUPS BATTER

For the batter amounts and baking times, see note below. You will need fifteen batches (or 86 cups) to make all the tiers. You can make separate batches for the larger layers.

8 tablespoons (1 stick) unsalted butter, at room temperature, plus more for the pans

¾ cup all-purpose flour, plus more for the pans

2½ ounces (½ cup) whole natural almonds, toasted

2½ ounces hazelnuts, toasted and skinned (½ cup)

¾ cup cake flour (not self-rising)

1½ teaspoons baking powder

¼ teaspoon salt

¼ cup granulated sugar

½ cup firmly packed dark brown sugar

2 teaspoons pure vanilla extract

¾ cup milk

4 large egg whites, at room temperature

1. Preheat the oven to 350°F. Brush the cake pans with butter. Line each with parchment; butter again, and dust with flour, tapping out any excess. Set aside.

2. In a food processor, finely grind the almonds and hazelnuts. Sift together the flours, baking powder, and salt into a medium bowl. Stir in the nuts, and set aside.

3. In the bowl of an electric mixer fitted with the whisk attachment, cream together the butter and sugars until smooth. Add the vanilla. On low speed, alternate adding the milk and the flour mixture, mixing well after each addition.

4. In a clean bowl with a clean whisk, whip the egg whites until soft peaks form. In two additions, fold the egg whites into the batter. Spread the batter into the prepared pans.

5. Bake the cakes until a skewer inserted into the centers comes out clean. Let cool in the pans on wire racks before unmolding. Store, well wrapped in plastic, at room temperature.

Approximate batter amounts and baking times for 2-inch-deep oval pans: 7¾ by 5⅝-inch: 3 cups, 35 minutes; 10¾ by 7⅝-inch: 6 cups, 40 minutes; 13 by 9⅞-inch: 9 cups, 45 minutes; 16½ by 12⅜-inch: 14 cups, 55 minutes

PISTACHIO BUTTERCREAM
MAKES ABOUT 7 CUPS

3 large eggs, separated

¾ cup sugar

1 cup whole milk

3 cups (6 sticks) unsalted butter, at room temperature

¾ cup pistachio paste

1. Combine the egg yolks and ¼ cup sugar in the bowl of an electric mixer fitted with the whisk attachment; beat on high speed until pale and thickened, 2 to 3 minutes.

2. Bring the milk to a boil in a medium saucepan. Remove from heat. Whisk about one third of the milk into the yolk mixture. Pour the mixture back into the pan with the remaining milk; whisk to combine. Cook over medium heat, stirring constantly, until the mixture registers 185°F on an instant-read thermometer. Remove from heat; strain. Refrigerate until cool.

3. Put the butter into the bowl of an electric mixer fitted with the paddle attachment; mix on medium-high speed until pale and fluffy. Mix in the chilled custard and the pistachio paste. Set aside.

4. Heat the egg whites and remaining ½ cup sugar in the clean heatproof bowl of an electric mixer set over a pan of simmering water, whisking constantly, until sugar has dissolved. Attach bowl to mixer fitted with the whisk attachment; beat on high speed until stiff peaks form.

5. Add the egg-white mixture to the butter mixture; beat on medium-high speed until smooth. Refrigerate in an airtight container for up to 3 days; bring to room temperature, and beat before using.

No. 39
TRANSFERWARE
CAKE

No. 40
HANDCRAFTED
HELLEBORE CAKE

{NO. 39} *Transferware, the nineteenth-century English pottery that inspired this cake, was known for intricate scenes and border patterns. Here, a border detail from a transferware plate is piped in chocolate, over and over again.*
{NO. 40} *A free-flowing ring of gum-paste hellebore flowers and leaves encircles this cake's middle tier. Two more blooms serve as a cake topper. The flowers are tinted sage green, chartreuse, and russet; fondant was mixed with marzipan to achieve the parchment hue of the cake layers. Mixing tier shapes creates visual interest.*

{NO. 41} *Meringue mushrooms sprout from snowy cake tiers iced in soft folds of Swiss meringue frosting. The mushrooms can be served alongside slices of the cake. To create different hues in the mushrooms, sprinkle a little cocoa powder into the meringue. See page 233 and 246 for the mushroom how-to and recipe.*

No. 42
COLORFUL
HYDRANGEA CAKE

No. 43
PERFECT PEAR
CAKE

{NO. 42} *This five-tier buttercream cake by Sylvia Weinstock is covered with sugar hydrangea blossoms in a progression of pinks.* {NO. 43} *On this fondant-covered cake, mini marzipan pears are positioned at different angles, as if they've just fallen from the tree onto the pristine tiers. When making the little fruits, scrape the seeds of a vanilla bean into the marzipan and knead to distribute and add color. Then snip the bean itself to use for the pears' stems.*

{NO. 44} *The delicate motifs on this pale-blue cake were imprinted using surprising tools: leather embossers. Two tiers are draped in garlands of tiny paper leaves and bows. A matching wreath topper symbolizes the eternal nature of marriage. The cake sits on a pedestal stand decorated with layers of scalloped tissue.*

{NO. 45} *Ladyfingers dressed in white circle the tiers of this cake. Decorated with pear blossoms, it's perfect for springtime, but any flowers can be used. The sides of the cookies are trimmed before they're iced so they'll fit snugly.*

No. 44

GARLANDS AND
WREATHS CAKE

No. 45

PICKET FENCE
CAKE

{NO. 46} *A simple cake frosted with white buttercream rises from a sea of blown-sugar bubbles that mimic both the color and the festive air of Champagne. The piped buttercream dots on the cake continue the playful theme.*
{NO. 47} *These shimmering platinum-blue bands and bow weren't woven from any cloth; they were pulled from sugar. The fondant-covered cake by Rémy Fünfrock is displayed on a hotel-silver tray.*

Crochet Plan
Row 1 – chain 10 close ring
" 2 – chain 9, 1 dbl. cr.
   in ring – * chain 6
   dble crochet in ring 6
   from * 3 t___ chain 6
   and j___ ___ 1ch ___
   1st c___
Row 3 –

CLARK

WEDDING ETIQUETTE
and
THE JEWELER

TARTINE
BAKE

No. 48

EYELET CAKE

Each fondant-covered tier of this cake presents a different eyelet, in both pattern and scale (hence the various proportions of the tiers). The second layer is inspired by the table runner; the cake's crown echoes the design of the bottom tier (which has a sugar-paste ribbon "threaded" through it). Deciding on the patterns for the other layers was more difficult, as there were many lovely samples to choose from (see photograph, opposite). The eyelet work was done on panels of fondant, which were pieced together around the tiers. The blue-and-white color scheme was in keeping with the vintage feel of the cake.

{NO. 49} *Each of these hydrangea blossoms is made of sugar paste. The dowels separating the cakes are covered with more of the flowers; sugared bay leaves complement the blue and purple hues of the flowers. A large leaf tip was used to pipe a decorative trim on the top and bottom of each tier.* {NO. 50} *A cluster of lavender, pink, and white blooms rests on top of this monochromatic monogrammed cake; the nosegay's luxurious taffeta ribbon trails down the side. The monogram and piped dots were hand-painted with luster dust for a subtle shimmer.*

No. 49
SUGAR HYDRANGEA
CAKE

No. 50
BERIBBONED
BOUQUET CAKE

PINK CHERRY BLOSSOM CAKE

SERVES ABOUT 150

When making the decorations, don't worry if you break a
few flowers. Individual petals look beautiful and realistic alongside the blooms.

*2 each 6-, 9-, 12-, and 15-inch by 2-inch-high hexagonal layers
of Chocolate Butter Cake (recipe follows)*

4 pieces corresponding-size ³⁄₁₆-inch-thick foam board

5 batches Chocolate-Cherry Ganache (recipe follows)

Cocoa powder, for dusting

12½ pounds chocolate fondant

1 rubber cake mat (6-inch diameter; optional)

1 cake board or platter (18-inch diameter)

26 wooden dowels (¼ inch in diameter, 4⅛ inches long)

1 batch Royal Icing (page 243)

Gum-Paste Cherry Blossoms (see page 227)

1. Prepare the tiers: Trim and split the layers. Brush the tops with the reduced liquid from the cherries. On corresponding-size foam boards, fill the layers with ganache to create 4-inch-tall tiers. Thinly coat with ganache (without cherries) to seal in the crumbs; chill until set, about 30 minutes.

2. Cover the tiers: On a work surface lightly dusted with cocoa powder, roll out the fondant for one tier at a time, about ⅛ inch thick. Working quickly, gently center the fondant on the tier. Using the palm of your hand, start from the center, and smooth it onto the tier. Trim the excess from the bottom edge with a pizza cutter.

3. Assemble the tiers: Place the cake mat or several drops of hot glue on the cake board; center and place the 15-inch tier on top. Insert 12 dowels into this tier (4 in a square in the center, and 8 in a circle about 2 inches from the edge), and dab royal icing on top of the tier. Center and place the 12-inch tier on top; insert 8 dowels in a circle, and dab royal icing on top. Center and place the 9-inch tier on top; insert 6 dowels in a circle about 1½ inches from the edge. Top with the 6-inch tier. Pipe small dots in the centers of the cherry blossoms using pale pink royal icing. Attach to the cake with brown royal icing.

*Approximate fondant amounts (12½ pounds total): 6-inch tier: 1½ pounds; 9-inch tier: 2½
pounds; 12-inch tier: 3½ pounds; 15-inch tier: 5 pounds*

"Depending on one's skill and patience, making these decorations and assembling the cake can take two to five days. Many people can't imagine the amount of time, skill, and passion that a wedding cake demands!"

Wendy

{NO. 51} *Cherry blossoms seem to float from the top of this cake down to the bottom, where the pink petals break apart as they would in nature.*

CHOCOLATE BUTTER CAKE
MAKES 6 CUPS BATTER

For batter amounts and baking times for the cake layers, see note below. You will need 46½ cups of batter for all four tiers; this recipe can be multiplied.

14 tablespoons (1¾ sticks) unsalted butter, at room temperature, plus more for the pans

2½ cups cake flour (not self-rising), sifted, plus more for the pans

¾ cup unsweetened Dutch-process cocoa powder

1½ tablespoons baking powder

¼ teaspoon salt

1 cup plus 2 tablespoons milk

1 tablespoon pure vanilla extract

1¾ cups sugar

5 large egg whites

1. Preheat the oven to 350°F. Brush the cake pans with butter. Line each with parchment paper; butter the parchment, and dust with flour, tapping out any excess. Set aside.

2. Sift together the flour, cocoa powder, baking powder, and salt into a medium bowl; set aside. Stir together the milk and vanilla; set aside. Put the butter in the bowl of an electric mixer fitted with the paddle attachment; beat on medium speed until pale and fluffy, about 3 minutes. Add the sugar in a steady stream; mix until pale and fluffy, about 3 minutes.

3. Reduce the speed to low. Add the flour mixture in three batches, alternating with the milk mixture and beginning and ending with the flour; mix until just combined.

4. Whisk the egg whites just until stiff peaks form. Fold the egg whites into the batter in three batches. Divide the batter among the prepared pans; smooth tops with an offset spatula. Firmly tap the pans on a work surface to release air bubbles.

5. Bake until a cake tester inserted into the centers comes out clean and the tops are springy to the touch. Let cool in the pans on wire racks for 15 minutes; turn out onto racks to cool completely, top sides up.

Approximate batter amounts and baking times for 2-inch-deep hexagonal pans: 6-inch: 1¾ cups, 30 minutes; 9-inch: 3½ cups, 35 minutes; 12-inch: 6 cups, 40 minutes; 15-inch: 12 cups, 50 minutes

CHOCOLATE-CHERRY GANACHE
MAKES 3 CUPS

This recipe makes both the filling and the coating for the tiers, as well as the kirsch syrup for brushing the cake layers. If desired, reduce more kirsch liquid for serving. You will need about 4 cups for crumb-coating the tiers; do not add cherries to this amount.

1¾ cups heavy cream

12 ounces best-quality semisweet chocolate, finely chopped

1½ cups drained kirsch-soaked cherries, cut in half, plus 2 cups liquid from jar

1. Bring the cream just to a boil, stirring occasionally, in a small saucepan over medium heat; remove from the heat. Put the chocolate in a medium heat-proof bowl, and pour the cream on top; let stand for 5 minutes. Gently stir until the ganache is smooth and glossy. Refrigerate the ganache, stirring occasionally, until slightly cooled and thickened, about 10 minutes (do not let it harden).

2. Meanwhile, chop the cherries in half; set aside. Cook the cherry liquid in a small saucepan over medium-low heat until reduced by half, about 10 minutes; set aside, covered, until ready to assemble the cake.

3. Gently fold the drained chopped cherries into the ganache (except for any used for crumb-coating the tiers). Let stand at room temperature, stirring occasionally, until spreadable.

{ARRANGING FLOWERS} *Martha uses tiny dots of royal icing to adhere the cherry blossoms to the cake. There are about 500 of them, enough to adorn each slice when the cake is served.*

No. 52
BEADED BOUQUET
CAKE

No. 53
TRIO OF SHELL
CAKES

{NO. 52} *Lovely crosshatching and beading, all crafted from fondant, resemble embroidery on a wedding dress; the bands of lush white flowers recall a bouquet.* {NO. 53} *These three masterful cakes are styled after "sailors' valentines"—keepsake boxes, decorated with intricate shell patterns, that nineteenth-century mariners created while at sea and then gave as gifts to their beloveds upon their return. Here, the shells—a total of about 1,500 of them!—are styled from gum paste and arranged in concentric circles, rosettes, and monograms.*

{NO. 54} *This cake by Susan Spungen is rich and dignified. The four ganache-coated tiers are garnished with glimmering sugared Seckel pears, crab apples, candied chestnuts, and other seasonal fruits.*

{NO. 55} *Smooth icing poppies and white-on-white patterns cover a square cake with cropped corners; gossamer ribbon brings out a hint of green in the fondant. The flowers were made using floodwork: A border was outlined and then filled in with royal icing, which has a fluid consistency. The blooms were transferred to fondant panels, which were then applied to the sides of the cake.* {NO. 56} *This cake by Florian Bellanger is named for a ski resort in the Alps and resembles a mountain covered in chocolate curls. Beneath them are disks of vanilla meringue layered with chocolate mousse.*

No. 55
ROYAL ICING
RELIEFS CAKE

No. 56
MEGÈVE CHOCOLATE
CAKE

Megève

{NO. 57} *Tiny wood-land beauties are rendered in marzipan on an ivory marzipan-covered cake. A ladybug, signifying good fortune, rests on the frond of a fern; a fiddle-head with royal-icing foliage uncoils overhead. Mushrooms with gum-paste stems, acorns, oak leaves, and fallen bark made of shaved chocolate further adorn the tiers.*

{NO. 58} *These gum-paste blossoms are meant to look more like silk flowers than real ones. At first glance, the cake appears to be monochromatic, but the edges of the petals are actually brushed with powdered coloring in a mix of moss green and pale pink.* {NO. 59} *Faux bois, the French term for "fake wood," refers to the wood-grain pattern on this dark and sophisticated cake. A wood-graining tool creates the white chocolate markings on bittersweet chocolate panels; they're then pressed into the chocolate ganache that envelops the cake. To make the leaves, tempered bittersweet chocolate is brushed onto real lemon leaves, which are peeled off after chilling briefly. See page 231 for faux bois how-to.*

No. 58
BLUSHING DOGWOOD
CAKE

No. 59
FAUX BOIS CAKE

{NO. 60} *The icing-like trim on jasperware, developed in England in 1775 by Josiah Wedgwood, translates well to a wedding cake. Porcelain-finish fondant is adorned with gum-paste leaves and flowers; the royal-icing ferns are created with a technique called brush embroidery, in which the wet icing is brushed for a feathery look.* {NO. 61} *Candies are scattered across tiers dusted in sparkling sugar; meringue powder mixed with water makes a sticky surface for the sugar to cling to. The sweets include rock candy, gumdrops, almond dragées, wafers, and chocolate candies.*

{NO. 62} *Silk-cord closures have been fashioned from rolled sugar paste and given a brushing of luster dust for the characteristic sheen. They line up along the sides of square tiers covered in fondant with a quilted pattern similar to those on the jackets the closures often adorn. Covering square tiers with fondant can be tricky for a novice—practice on foam squares to hone your skills.*

{NO. 63} *Tiers covered in white fondant are an excellent canvas for paper ornaments handmade by designer Denise Sharp. Crisply folded fans and stars are attached to the cake with royal icing. The banner on the second tier notes the couple's initials. Decorative black-and-white ribbons encircle the tiers and cake board.*

No. 62
SILK-CORD
ACCENTS CAKE

No. 63
PAPER ORNAMENT
CAKE

{NO. 64} *Clusters of spiky "petals" of soft meringue top the layers of this exuberant cake. The same icing, spread smooth, covers the sides. Soft meringues like this should be applied just before displaying the cake.* {NO. 65} *The graphic design on this dramatic cake is fashioned from different sizes of chocolate nonpareil candies—about 600 of them (buy extra so you can select pristine ones). They are attached to the fondant coating with dots of royal icing.*

No. 64

MERINGUE
CHRYSANTHEMUM
CAKE

No. 65

PATTERNED
NONPAREIL CAKE

{NO. 66} *When Darcy Miller,* Martha Stewart Weddings *editorial director, married Andy Nussbaum, they wanted a fantasy of a dessert, and based their nine-tier fondant-covered cake on Parisian bakery boxes. The tiers are delineated with chocolate beading and embellished with chocolate leaves, garlands, wreaths, and a monogram. Andy loves sweets, so they surrounded the cake with favorite candies and French macaroons. Guests at the wedding were also treated to miniature fondant-covered cakes by Sylvia Weinstock.*

{NO. 67} *The tops of these three stacked boxes are covered with fondant and marzipan buttons, some painted with a pale, shimmery coloring to simulate a pearly finish. At the base of each box is a fondant ribbon, made by pressing strips of fondant into ribbed elastic for the look of grosgrain. A gumpaste bow serves as the cake topper. For the cake table, grosgrain ribbons are woven together to cover a board.*

{NO. 68} *These pretty little cakes by Ron Ben-Israel—a fresh alternative to a single grand confection—are adorned with sprigs of sugar freesia in yellow, lavender, and white. The cakes are iced in the same colors but are paired with a differently hued flower. A Swiss-dot motif piped onto the fondant is echoed in the cloth draping the table.*

No. 67
BUTTON-TOPPED
BOXES CAKE

No. 68
TRIO OF
FREESIA CAKES

CHOCOLATE PETAL CAKE

SERVES 105

If ever there was a reason to work with chocolate in a warm room, this is it—
a moderately warm temperature makes it easier to curl the petals. However, the finished
cake must be stored away from direct heat or sunlight.

*1 each 6-, 10-, and 14-inch round contoured
layer of Mocha Spice Cake (recipe follows)*

3 pieces corresponding-size 3/16-inch-thick foam board

1 batch Ginger-Infused Simple Syrup (page 245)

2 batches Chocolate Buttercream (recipe follows)

1 cake board (20-inch diameter, 2 inches thick)

6 feet of 2-inch-wide ribbon

6 feet of 1/4-inch-wide ribbon

16 wooden dowels (1/4 inch in diameter, 4 1/8 inches long)

Chocolate Petals (page 244)

Sugared pansies and Johnny-jump-ups (see Sources, page 254)

1. Prepare the tiers: Trim and split each cake layer into thirds. On corresponding-size boards, brush the layers with simple syrup, and fill with buttercream to create 4-inch-tall tiers. Thinly coat with buttercream to seal in the crumbs; chill until set, about 30 minutes. Frost the tiers with more buttercream; refrigerate until ready to stack.

2. Prepare the cake board: Remove the 14-inch tier from the refrigerator; center and place on the cake board. Spread the board with buttercream; clean the edges. Using a hot-glue gun, attach the wide ribbon to the side of the board; glue the narrow ribbon onto the wide one.

3. Assemble the tiers: Insert 10 dowels vertically into the 14-inch tier, making a circle with 6 dowels about 2 inches from the edge and placing 4 in a square within the circle. Center and place the 10-inch tier on top. Insert the remaining 6 dowels in the 10-inch tier, in a circle about 2½ inches from the edge. Center and place the 6-inch tier on top.

4. Decorate the tiers: Fit a 12-inch pastry bag with a coupler and round (Ateco #5) tip; fill with buttercream. Attach the chocolate petals to the cake and cake board by piping a small amount of buttercream on the back of each petal. Decorate with sugared flowers.

"The petals for this cake can be made in a fraction of the time it would take to craft a bunch of gum-paste blossoms. Rather than painstakingly forming each one by hand, the petals are easily scraped from a block of chocolate."

Martha

{NO. 69} *Hidden beneath bittersweet chocolate curls and a smattering of edible sugared pansies are three tiers of Mocha Spice Cake frosted with chocolate buttercream. Cake by Claire Perez.*

MOCHA SPICE CAKE
MAKES 9 CUPS BATTER

For approximate batter amounts and baking times, see note below. You will need to make this recipe 3½ times for all the tiers. For even layers, bake each one separately.

1 cup (2 sticks) unsalted butter,
at room temperature, plus more for the pans

¾ cup Dutch-process cocoa powder, plus more for the pans

3 cups packed light-brown sugar

4 large eggs

2 teaspoons pure vanilla extract

2 tablespoons freshly grated ginger

2 teaspoons ground ginger

1½ teaspoons ground cinnamon

¼ teaspoon ground nutmeg

¼ teaspoon ground cloves

1 tablespoon baking soda

½ teaspoon salt

3 cups cake flour (not self-rising), sifted

1 cup sour cream

1½ cups hot coffee

1. Place a rack in the middle of the oven, and preheat the oven to 325°F. Brush the cake pans with butter. Line each with parchment paper; butter again, and dust with cocoa powder, tapping out any excess. Set aside.

2. In the bowl of an electric mixer fitted with the paddle attachment, cream the butter on medium until light. Add the brown sugar and eggs; beat on medium-high until fluffy, about 2 minutes. Add the vanilla, cocoa, fresh ginger, ground ginger, cinnamon, nutmeg, cloves, baking soda, and salt; mix well.

3. With the mixer on low, add a third of the flour; mix just until combined. Add half of the sour cream; mix. Repeat with the remaining flour and sour cream, ending with flour. Pour the coffee into the batter; mix until smooth.

4. Pour the batter into the prepared pans. Bake, rotating 90 degrees halfway through baking, until the sides start to pull away from the pans and a few crumbs remain on a cake tester that has been inserted into the centers and removed. Let cool in the pans on wire racks for 15 minutes. Invert and remove parchment. Let cool completely, right sides up.

Approximate batter amounts and baking times for 3-inch-deep contoured pans: 6-inch: 3½ cups, 75 minutes; 10-inch: 10 cups, 1 hour 50 minutes; 14-inch: 18 cups, 2 hours 10 minutes

CHOCOLATE BUTTERCREAM
MAKES 12 CUPS

We used Guanaja 70 percent bittersweet chocolate by Callebaut for its deep flavor and dark color.

24 ounces bittersweet chocolate, chopped

2½ cups sugar

10 large egg whites

2 pounds (8 sticks) unsalted butter, cut into pieces,
at room temperature

1. Place the chopped chocolate in a heat-proof bowl or in the top of a double boiler; set over a pan of simmering water. Stir until melted, remove from the heat. Stir occasionally until completely cooled. Set aside.

2. Combine the sugar and egg whites in the heat-proof bowl of an electric mixer. Place the bowl over a pan of simmering water; whisk until the mixture feels hot to the touch and the sugar is completely dissolved, about 3 minutes. Transfer the bowl to the mixer stand. Using the whisk attachment, beat the mixture on medium-high until cooled, about 15 minutes.

3. Add the butter pieces, one at a time, stirring constantly until incorporated. Add the cooled chocolate; stir well. Use the buttercream immediately, or transfer to an airtight container and refrigerate for up to 3 days. Bring to room temperature and stir with a rubber spatula before using.

{SWEET SERVING} *This flower girl's gingham dress matches the color of the sugared flowers that embellish the cake. (Use only edible flowers for presentations such as this; see pages 224–225 for more information.) Extra chocolate petals were made to be served alongside each slice. The cake's layers are rich and flavorful, as they contain cocoa powder, coffee, sour cream, and a mélange of fragrant spices. Using excellent-quality chocolate in the buttercream and for the petals makes every bite even more delectable.*

{NO. 70} *A chocolate sampler inspired this cake. Bands of tempered white chocolate piped with royal icing mimic a box shape; hand-molded truffles line the tiers. Beneath the chocolate bands, the sides of the cake can be iced with buttercream, but the tops are covered with fondant so the individual truffles can be lifted and served easily.*

{NO. 71} *A six-tier, fondant-covered wedding cake by Oheka Catering of Huntington, New York, is decorated with sprightly crepe-paper flowers and given a skirt of crepe paper, pleats stitched in place.*

No. 70
CANDY SAMPLER
CAKE

No. 71
PLAYFUL PAPER
FLOWER CAKE

Miniature chocolate and vanilla cupcakes surround white-fondant tiers speckled with piped Swiss dots. The smart brown-and-white color scheme is anything but homespun; the precise dimensions of the cake give it a pulled-together look. (See opposite for our calculations as we planned.) The paper flags waving from piped icing swirls feature various ornate patterns inspired by transferware china or toile fabric; the ones at top are calligraphed with the newlyweds' names.

{NO. 73} *The stylized relief work on this stacked cake is sculpted from marzipan using traditional German cookie forms called springerle molds; the central medallion depicts a bride and groom emerging from a sunflower. Piped icing borders hide the seams between panels.* {NO. 74} *The classic American layer cake is dressed up with geraniums for an informal wedding. The chocolate frosting is spread on the cake in broad strokes that require no special decorating skills. The colorful flowers are tucked into trays filled with floral foam.*

No. 75
CHARMING
CALICO CAKE

{NO. 75} *Printed fabric has been reinterpreted on a cake with approximately 800 diminutive hand-sculpted flowers, leaves, and fruits. Set against ivory fondant, the gum-paste strawberries and cherries grow from stems of piped royal icing, tinted brown. Real rickrack trim, secured with royal icing, emphasizes the cake's fabric origin.*

DEVIL'S FOOD FINALE CAKE

SERVES ABOUT 380

With its seven towering tiers, this cake is best assembled at the reception site.
It would be heavy and cumbersome for even two people to carry.

2 each 6-, 8-, 10-, 12-, 14-, 16-, and 18-inch round layers
of Devil's Food Cake (23½ batches total; recipe follows)

7 pieces corresponding-size ³⁄₁₆-inch-thick foam board

11 batches Italian Meringue (recipe follows)

1 round cake board or stand (20-inch diameter)

39 wooden dowels (¼ inch in diameter, approximately 4⅛ inches long)

Chocolate Sauce, for serving (recipe follows)

1. Prepare the tiers: Trim and split the layers. On corresponding-size foam boards, fill the layers with meringue to create 4-inch-tall tiers, and coat the top and sides with more meringue, swooping the sides decoratively.

2. Assemble the tiers: Center and place the 18-inch tier on the cake board. Insert 1 dowel in the center of the 18-inch tier and 9 dowels evenly spaced in a circle, about 2½ inches from the edge. Follow the same procedure for the remaining tiers: Insert 8 dowels in the 16-inch tier; 7 dowels in the 14-inch tier; 5 dowels in the 12-inch tier; 5 dowels in the 10-inch tier; and 4 dowels in the 8-inch tier (1 in the center and the rest evenly spaced, about 1½ inches from the edge). Stack the tiers from largest to smallest.

3. To serve, place slices on plates; spoon chocolate sauce over.

> "If you lean toward a classic, elegant look but crave a little drama, consider a cake like this, with rich devil's food layers beneath traditional white icing."
>
> *Wendy*

{NO. 76} *A sweet flower girl sneaks a taste of the Italian meringue that covers this cake. From its pristine white appearance, you wouldn't guess that rich devil's food is inside. If you are planning a smaller wedding but still want a grand cake like this, substitute some foam tiers for cake tiers.*

DEVIL'S FOOD CAKE
MAKES 8 CUPS BATTER

For approximate batter amounts and baking times, see note below; this recipe can be multiplied. You will need a total of 188 cups of batter for all seven tiers.

1½ cups (3 sticks) unsalted butter, at room temperature, plus more for the pans

3 cups cake flour (not self-rising), sifted

¾ cup Dutch-process cocoa powder, plus more for the pans

½ cup boiling water

2¼ cups sugar

1 tablespoon pure vanilla extract

4 large eggs, lightly beaten

1 teaspoon baking soda

½ teaspoon salt

1 cup whole milk

1. Preheat the oven to 350°F. Brush the cake pans with butter. Line each with parchment paper; butter the parchment, and dust with cocoa powder, tapping out any excess. Set aside. Stir together the cocoa powder and boiling water in a small heat-proof bowl until a smooth paste forms. Let cool.

2. Mix the butter and sugar in the bowl of an electric mixer fitted with the paddle attachment until pale and fluffy, 3 to 4 minutes. Mix in the vanilla. Add the eggs in a slow stream, mixing until the batter is no longer slick.

3. Sift together the flour, baking soda, and salt into a large bowl. Gradually whisk the milk into the reserved cocoa paste. With the mixer on low, gradually add the flour and cocoa mixtures. Divide among the prepared pans. Bake, rotating the pans halfway through, until a cake tester inserted into the centers comes out clean. Let cool in the pans on wire racks for 5 to 10 minutes before turning out onto racks; let cool completely.

Approximate batter amounts and baking times for 2-inch-deep round pans: 6-inch: 2 cups, 35 minutes; 8-inch: 4 cups, 40 minutes; 10-inch: 6 cups, 50 minutes; 12-inch: 10 cups, 60 minutes; 14-inch: 16 cups, 70 minutes; 16-inch: 24 cups, 80 minutes; 18-inch: 32 cups, 90 minutes

ITALIAN MERINGUE
MAKES ABOUT 8 CUPS

Because the meringue dries quickly, it is better to make it in small batches, so do not double this recipe.

2¾ cups granulated sugar

9 large egg whites

½ teaspoon cream of tartar

1 cup sifted confectioners' sugar

1. Bring the granulated sugar and ⅔ cup water to a boil in a small saucepan, swirling the pan to dissolve the sugar. Wash down the sides of the pan with a wet pastry brush to prevent crystals from forming. Boil until the syrup registers 238°F on a candy thermometer.

2. Meanwhile, in the bowl of an electric mixer fitted with the whisk, beat the egg whites on low speed until foamy. Add the cream of tartar; mix on medium-high until stiff but not dry.

3. With the mixer running, slowly pour in the hot sugar syrup; mix on high until the mixture has partially cooled, 5 to 7 minutes. Reduce the speed to medium; slowly add the confectioners' sugar. Raise the speed to medium-high; mix until completely cool, 7 to 10 minutes. Use immediately.

CHOCOLATE SAUCE
MAKES ABOUT 2½ CUPS

You will need at least ten batches to serve with the cake. This recipe can be multiplied.

12 ounces best-quality semisweet chocolate, coarsely chopped

2 cups heavy cream

Place the chocolate in a heat-proof bowl. Heat the cream in a saucepan over high heat until almost boiling; pour over the chocolate. Let stand for 5 minutes, then stir until smooth. Refrigerate until thickened but still pourable, stirring occasionally.

{NO. 77} *Roses piped in pink, peach, and yellow encircle a dainty cake. The flowers' variegated look is achieved by placing two colors of icing side by side in the pastry bag. Dots are piped in the same buttercream that covers the tiers.*
{NO. 78} *Against white fondant, a wreath of flowers—among them, fringed nerines and primula in pink, tiny yellow kalanchoe, and papery sweet peas—is even more glorious. The cake base rests within a ring of floral foam; space in between keeps the flowers from touching the icing. The top tier is Styrofoam, providing support for the weighty bouquet.*

No. 77

ROSE GARDEN
CAKE

No. 78

GARDEN OF SWEET
DELIGHTS CAKE

No. 79
LEMON AND
LATTICEWORK CAKE

No. 80
DELIGHTFUL
DAISIES CAKE

{NO. 79} *Royal-icing latticework gives this cake a summery feel, but the year-round appeal of citrus fruit makes it right for any season. The 240 lemons are actually tinted white chocolate; the 70 blossoms, gum paste; and the 120 leaves, white fondant.*

{NO. 80} *Gum-paste daisies drift down a fondant-covered cake by Gail Watson. This cascading effect is created by covering the top tier entirely with the blooms and placing fewer and fewer on the bottom tiers. The choice of daisies, a decidedly old-fashioned flower, gives the simple, modern design a retro appeal. The cake's petite form gains presence when displayed on a footed cake stand.*

No. 81

CANDY STRAW
CAKE

This cake seems plucked from an old-fashioned candy shop, with its dreamy pastels and confectionary decorations. Mimicking a traditional charlotte, the tiers are encircled by approximately 250 strawberry-, lemon-, and lime-flavored candy straws that are filled with chocolate. The wrapping from a favorite New York spot inspired the gold-flecked pink ribbons that finish each tier with a dainty bow. A pink milk-glass cake stand echoes the palette as well as the nostalgic mood.

PINK MADELEINE CAKE

SERVES UP TO 100

Bake extra madeleines as favors for your guests.
Package them with the same ribbon that adorns the cake.

*2 each 6-, 8-, 10-, and 12-inch-round by 2-inch-high
layers Vanilla-Bean Sponge Cake (recipe follows)*

4 pieces corresponding-size ³⁄₁₆-inch-thick foam board

1 recipe Lemon Simple Syrup (page 75)

*2 batches Swiss Meringue Buttercream (page 238), tinted with pink
gel-paste food coloring (such as Baker's Rose or Old Rose)*

1 cake stand or platter (14-inch diameter)

18 wooden dowels (¼ inch in diameter, 4⅛ inches long)

2 batches Lemon Madeleines (page 246)

10 yards ⅛-inch-wide gold metallic ribbon

1. Prepare the tiers: Trim and split the layers. On corresponding-size foam boards, brush the layers with simple syrup, and fill with buttercream to create 4-inch-tall tiers. Thinly coat with buttercream to seal in the crumbs; chill until set, about 30 minutes. Remove one tier from the refrigerator. Place on a turntable and coat smoothly with buttercream. Return to the refrigerator. Repeat with the remaining tiers.

2. Assemble the tiers: Center and place the 12-inch tier on the cake stand. Insert 8 dowels in a circle 2½ inches from the edge. Center and place the 10-inch tier on top; insert 6 dowels in a circle 2½ inches from the edge. Center and place the 8-inch tier on top; insert 4 dowels in a square 2½ inches from the edge. Center and place the 6-inch tier on top. Using a star tip (such as Ateco #16), pipe reverse shell borders on the top edges of all the tiers. Refrigerate.

3. Decorate the cake: Apply madeleines by piping a dab of buttercream onto the back of each, then securing to the tiers. Wrap a ribbon around each tier, using a hot-glue gun to secure the ends (in the back of the cake). Use glue to attach bows to the ribbon on every other madeleine.

{NO. 82} *The lemon-flavored cookie-like madeleines are nestled against shell-pink buttercream tiers and wrapped with gold ribbon—every other one finished with a bow. The citrus taste is carried over to the light and airy sponge cake, which is brushed with lemon syrup.*

"My daughter, Alexis, is a very fine baker, and when she saw this photograph, she was inspired to re-create the cake at home. She loves the simple sponge cookies called madeleines and the pretty pink icing."

Martha

VANILLA-BEAN SPONGE CAKE

MAKES 7 CUPS BATTER

For approximate batter amounts and baking times,
see note below. This recipe can be doubled. You will need
28½ cups of batter for the four tiers.

8 tablespoons (1 stick) unsalted butter, cut into ½-inch pieces,
plus more for the pans

2½ cups cake flour (not self-rising), sifted,
plus more for the pans

½ cup milk

4 whole vanilla beans

1½ teaspoons baking powder

6 large whole eggs, at room temperature

6 large egg yolks, at room temperature

1 teaspoon pure vanilla extract

1¾ cups sugar

1. Preheat the oven to 325°F. Brush the cake pans with butter.
Line each with parchment paper; butter again, and dust with
all-purpose flour, tapping out any excess. Set aside.

2. Place the milk in a double boiler. Slice the vanilla beans in
half lengthwise; scrape the seeds into the milk, and add the
vanilla pods. Heat over very low heat until the milk is just
warm, about 2 minutes. Remove from the heat, cover, and let
steep for 15 minutes. Add the butter and return to very low
heat just until the butter melts.

3. Meanwhile, sift the cake flour and baking powder together
twice into a bowl; set aside.

4. Combine the whole eggs, egg yolks, and vanilla extract in
the heat-proof bowl of an electric mixer fitted with the whisk
attachment. Beat to combine, then whisk in the sugar. Place
the mixing bowl over the double boiler; heat over medium-low
heat until the sugar dissolves and the mixture is just warm to
the touch, 5 to 7 minutes.

5. Return the bowl to the electric mixer; whisk on high speed
until cooled and thick enough to hold a ribbon on the surface,
9 to 10 minutes. (To test: Lift the beater from the mixture, and
draw a figure eight by dripping batter from the beater; the
batter is ready when the pattern stays on the surface for 3 seconds.) Using a rubber spatula, fold the flour mixture into the
egg mixture in three additions.

6. Strain the milk mixture through a sieve into a large bowl.
Gradually mix 1½ cups of the egg mixture into the milk mixture. Fold this mixture into the remaining egg mixture. Divide
the batter among the prepared pans.

7. Bake until a cake tester inserted into the centers comes out
clean. Transfer to wire racks; let cool in the pans for 30 minutes. Invert the cakes onto racks. Remove the parchment;
reinvert the cakes top sides up. The cakes can be wrapped in
plastic and stored at room temperature for up to 1 day.

Approximate batter amounts and baking times for 3-inch-deep
round pans: 6-inch: 3½ cups, 40 minutes; 8-inch: 5½ cups,
45 minutes; 10-inch: 8½ cups, 50 minutes; 12-inch: 11 cups,
1 hour 10 minutes

{FINISHING TOUCH} *Wendy and Martha use buttercream to*
"glue" madeleines to the cake layers. The last step will be adding
thin gold ribbon around the tiers—for that, real glue will be used.

No. 83

WEDDING BAND
CAKE

No. 84

RUSTIC ROSES
CAKE

{NO. 83} *These white tiers were dressed with metallic ribbons to mimic nineteenth-century wedding-band china, which was shipped plain from France and trimmed with gold paint once it reached the United States. Sprigs of fresh olive branches add a soft, natural finish to the cake.* {NO. 84} *This decadent confection, made by Elizabeth Loudon, a cousin of the groom at this wedding, is covered with whorls of bittersweet chocolate frosting and dressed with roses and fiddleheads. It rests on a felt-trimmed stand.*

Five cakes festooned with tuile cookies bearing words of love make an enticing buffet. From left: Toasted-coconut frosting coats feather-light angel's food cake. Sliced almonds march around the sides of a rectangular dacquoise cake with ganache. A diminutive French croquembouche—the traditional French wedding cake—is built from profiteroles and given a halo of spun sugar (see recipe and how-tos on pages 247–250). A heart-shaped chocolate-glazed cake rests on candied orange slices. Brown-sugar buttercream covers a three-tier cake.

{NO. 86} *In an ode to early summer, fresh strawberries are piled high on stacked pound cakes with mascarpone cream sandwiched between the layers. Platters piped with royal icing in a basket-weave pattern lend a country feel; they sit on ribbon-wrapped columns that elevate the dessert from its rustic origins and allude to the shape of a conventional tiered wedding cake.*

{NO. 87} *This three-tiered buttercream cake by Samantha Connell celebrates nature's finest bounty with boughs of fresh fruit and sprigs of currants. The clean lines of the wooden board below emphasize the cake's unfussy structure.*

No. 86
STRAWBERRY
SHORTCAKE

No. 87
FARMSTAND FRUIT AND
BUTTERCREAM CAKE

{NO. 88} *In a creation that is fun but still elegant, dots of ivory fondant cover a coating of pure white fondant.*
The chic confection, by April Reed Cake Design, has unusual proportions: Its extra-tall lower tiers give it height
and a modern look. {NO. 89} *Four buttercream cubes topped with brilliant parrot tulips glow with color;*
every cluster picks up a hue from the one next to it. To prevent marring the soft icing, the blooms are arranged on clear
acetate sheets. Each cake serves sixty; for easier slicing, foam board separates the two four-inch-high layers.

No. 88
IVORY DOTS CAKE

No. 89
PARROT-TULIP
QUARTET OF CAKES

No. 90
BLOOMING
BRANCHES CAKE

No. 91
CASCADING
ORCHIDS CAKE

{NO. 90} *Delicate sugar cherry blossoms on wire stems seem to come to life as they wind gracefully around the tiers of a diminutive fondant-covered cake by Sylvia Weinstock.* {NO. 91} *Dozens of sugar-paste orchids flow from the base to the top of a five-tier cake by Ron Ben-Israel. The flowers have the depth and detail of real ones, and they seem to glow against the backdrop of pale-pink fondant.*

{NO. 92} *Sophisticated and flirty, this cake is reminiscent of the classic French charlotte. Dark modeling chocolate wraps each tier; the edges are scalloped to resemble ladyfingers. Pink velvet ribbon complements the texture of the chocolate, and each layer glistens with tinted sanding sugar. See page 230 for chocolate band how-to.* {NO. 93} *Dainty sprigs of lily-of-the-valley crafted from sugar spring from the tiers of this little cake—just twelve inches tall—by Ron Ben-Israel. More flowers are piped in royal icing onto the soft-white fondant covering the cake.*

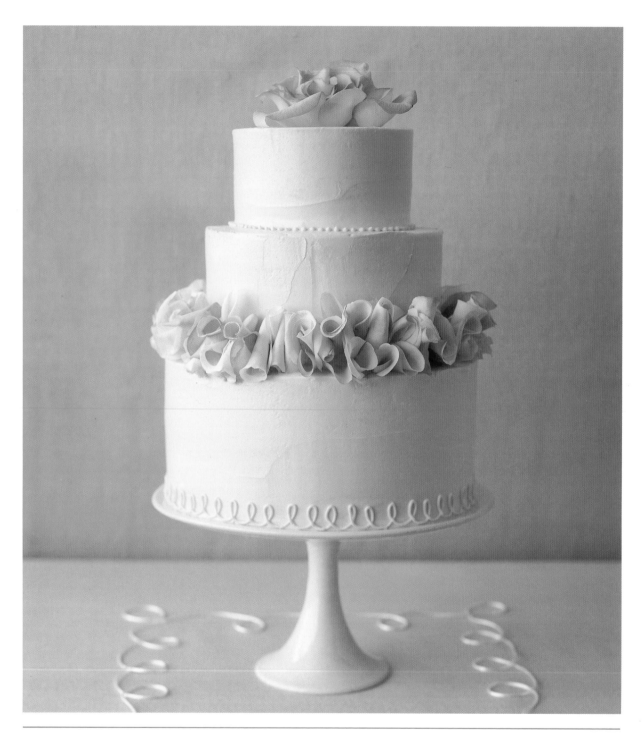

{NO. 94} *White chocolate buttercream tinted yellow makes a pretty backdrop for a string of rose petals in soft shades of cream and blushing yellow. To make the garland, remove petals from roses; stack three petals and roll into a loose cylinder. Insert craft wire through the roll, and repeat, adding until the garland is the desired length. The topper is a single bloom with its sepal removed so the petals fall open.* {NO. 95} *Black lace licorice is wrapped around pristine fondant-covered tiers for an effect that is tailored, modern, and sophisticated.*

No. 94
RUFFLY ROSE-PETAL
GARLAND CAKE

No. 95
LOVELY LICORICE
CAKE

No. 96
CHOCOLATE
KUMQUAT CAKE

No. 97
CITRUS BASKET
CAKE

{NO. 96} *The oval tiers of this chocolate cake by Claire Perez are spaced, giving a feeling of lightness to the rich confection. They are covered in whipped ganache, then wrapped in bands of tempered bittersweet chocolate. The bands are adorned with flowers cut from kumquat skins and with leaves and flourishes piped in dark and white chocolate.* {NO. 97} *Hexagonal tiers supported by a center pedestal are piped with "wicker-work" buttercream. Sugared kumquats and their leaves, as well as gum-paste orange blossoms, peek out from between the tiers.*

{NO. 98} *Clusters of marzipan cherries adorn a three-tier cake, by Wendy and Bill Yosses, covered in rolled-out marzipan.*
A baker should plan on making the cherries at least a week in advance, as they need time to firm up. (See page 243
for marzipan how-to.) Cherries and almonds are close botanical relatives, and they're famously compatible in desserts,
so a filling of sour cherry jam was chosen to complement the flavor of marzipan.

{NO. 99} *This ladylike cake is a celebration of 1950s fashion, when couture Dior (with its buttons and bows) was in vogue. We started by gathering black-and-white ribbons, then tying them into tailored bows for Wendy to replicate in sugar paste. Clever use of a perforation wheel makes it appear as if the ribbons have been stitched onto the fondant-covered tiers. The outlining of black food coloring, which helps define the white-on-white shapes, was painted on by hand (which we knew would be no easy task, as evidenced by the plea with Wendy on one of numerous sketches). The stylish color scheme is carried out on the extra-thick cake board, which is covered in aqua paper and black-and-white ribbon.*

No. 99

RIBBONS AND
BOWS CAKE

RED VELVET CAKE

SERVES 175

Red velvet cake is a Southern classic, so we chose to adorn
this multitiered version with magnolias, another favorite of the South.

3 each 6-, 9-, 12-, and 15-inch round layers,
plus two 4-inch round layers, of Red Velvet Cake (recipe follows)

5 pieces corresponding-size 3/16-inch-thick foam board

5 batches Cream Cheese Frosting (recipe follows)

1 cake board (18-inch diameter)

25 wooden dowels (1/4 inch in diameter, 4 1/8 inches long)

3 gum-paste magnolias (see Sources, page 254)

1. Prepare the tiers: Trim the layers. On corresponding-size foam boards, fill 6-, 9-, 12-, and 15-inch layers with frosting to create 4-inch-tall tiers. Repeat with the 4-inch layers to make a 3-inch-high tier. Frost the tiers.

2. Decorate the tiers by pressing a large offset spatula vertically against the sides at 1-inch intervals to make swooping ridges. Chill until icing is firm.

3. Assemble the tiers: Center and place the 15-inch tier on the cake board. Insert 10 dowels, arranging 1 in the center and 9 in a circle 2½ inches from the edge. Center and place the 12-inch tier on top; insert 8 dowels in a circle 2½ inches from the edge. Center and place the 9-inch tier on top; insert 4 dowels in a square 2½ inches from the edge. Center and place the 6-inch tier on top; insert the last 3 dowels in a triangle 2 inches from the edge. Place the 4-inch tier on top. Refrigerate the cake until ready to display. Decorate with gum-paste magnolias.

"This cake offers a very big surprise when the white icing is cut through with a knife, revealing the vivid red cake inside. The simple, elegant tiers and opulent gum-paste magnolias belie the cake's true simplicity."

Martha

{NO. 100} *Underneath the swooping white frosting of this tiered dessert are scarlet layers infused with buttermilk and cocoa. For added flavor, we've used a tangy cream cheese frosting, spreading it between the layers and outside of the cake.*

RED VELVET CAKE
MAKES 10 CUPS BATTER

For approximate batter amounts and baking times, see note below. You will need 10 batches of batter; this recipe can be multiplied. Fill and bake three each of the 6-, 9-, 12-, and 15-inch pans; trim to make 1¼-inch-high layers. Fill and bake two 4-inch pans; trim both to make 1½-inch-high layers.

Unsalted butter, at room temperature, for the pans

¼ cup Dutch-process cocoa powder,
plus more for the pans

5 cups cake flour (not self-rising), sifted

2 teaspoons salt

3 cups sugar

3 cups canola oil

4 large eggs

¾ teaspoon red gel-paste food coloring

2 teaspoons pure vanilla extract

2 cups low-fat buttermilk

1 tablespoon baking soda

4 teaspoons white vinegar

1. Preheat the oven to 350°F. Brush the cake pans with butter. Line each with parchment paper; butter the parchment, and dust with cocoa powder, tapping out any excess. Set aside. Whisk together the flour, salt, and cocoa powder in a medium bowl; set aside.

2. In the bowl of an electric mixer fitted with the whisk attachment, mix the sugar and oil on medium speed until combined. Add the eggs one at a time; mix well after each addition. Mix in the food coloring and vanilla. Add the flour mixture in three batches, alternating with the buttermilk and beginning and ending with flour, mixing well after each addition. Scrape down the sides of the bowl as needed.

3. Stir together the baking soda and vinegar in a small bowl. Add the baking-soda mixture to the batter, and mix on medium speed for 10 seconds. Pour the batter into the prepared pans. Bake until a cake tester inserted into the centers comes out clean. Let cool completely in the pans on wire racks.

Approximate batter amounts and baking times for 3-inch-deep round pans: 4-inch: 1½ cups, 25 minutes; 6-inch: 3¼ cups, 45 minutes; 9-inch: 5 cups, 50 minutes; 12-inch: 9 cups, 1 hour; 15-inch: 13 cups, 1 hour 15 minutes

CREAM CHEESE FROSTING
MAKES 8 CUPS

2 pounds (four 8-ounce packages) cream cheese,
at room temperature

1 teaspoon pure vanilla extract

8 tablespoons (1 stick) unsalted butter, at room temperature,
cut into pieces

2 pounds confectioners' sugar, sifted

---

1. In the bowl of an electric mixer fitted with the paddle attachment, mix the cream cheese and vanilla on medium speed until creamy and light, 2 minutes. With the mixer running, gradually add the butter; mix until combined.

2. Reduce the speed to low; gradually mix in the confectioners' sugar until combined. If not using immediately, refrigerate, covered, for up to 3 days; bring to room temperature and beat until smooth before using.

{NO. 101} *This five-tier cake is a graphic interpretation of damask fabric; it plays up the pattern, which is traditionally tone-on-tone. The scrollwork is best suited to a square cake because the flat surfaces display the repeating motif to greatest advantage. Wendy attaches the delicate flourishes to the cake by piping on dabs of royal icing. She always makes extra sets of scrollwork to allow for breakage. (See page 233 for the damask how-to.)*

No. 102
VINTAGE MONOGRAM
CAKE

No. 103
PIN TUCKS AND
RUFFLES CAKE

{NO. 102} *A simple square cake is a literal translation of a wonderful old letter found in a vintage-paper and print shop. The royal-icing monogram is surrounded by a rolled-fondant flower garland on a blue background. (See page 217 for the monogram how-to.)*

{NO. 103} *Two classic fabric flourishes— pin tucks and ruffles— encircle the layers of this formal cake. Tiny gum-paste pearls, like fabric-covered buttons, punctuate the center of each frilly sugar-paste band. Taffeta ribbon trims the cake board. A pasta-rolling machine is a great help when making the dozens of bands for this cake.*

{NO. 106} *Fondant that has been tinted ice blue blankets this cake, which would be a stunning choice at a winter wedding with modern style. Real pinecones flocked with royal icing and glistening with sanding sugar are accented with finely wrought chocolate pine needles, adding a natural-looking texture to the cake's modern lines. An overhead view of the three-tier cake (opposite) shows off the graphic pattern of the "pine needles."*

No. 104
SNOW-FLECKED
PINECONES CAKE

No. 105
SHOWERED-IN-WHITE
CAKE

No. 106
BAMBOO WAVE
CAKE

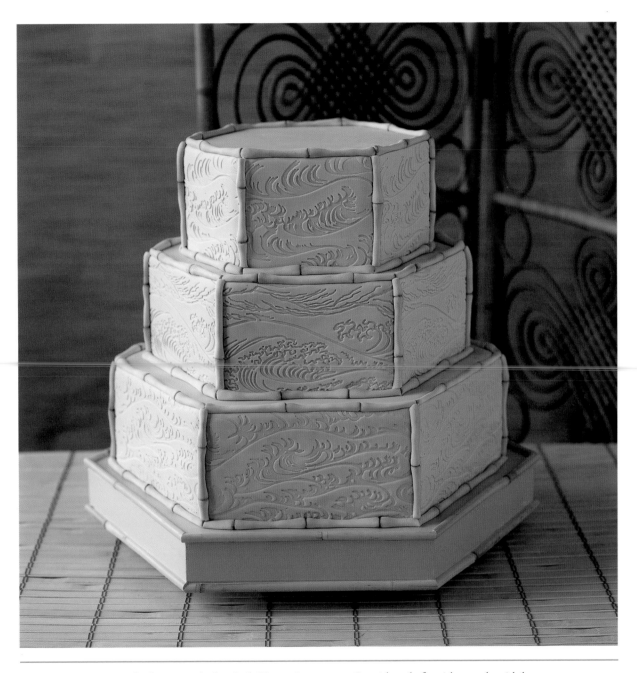

{NO. 105} *The four-tier cake by Gail Watson incorporates Spanish-style flourishes made with buttercream.
The cake is topped with a glass compote holding cards on which promises are written.* {NO. 106} *A different wave design
(made by imprinting fondant with a rubber stamp) graces each panel of this ocean-inspired cake. (See pages
214–215 for fondant and imprinting how-tos.) Every panel is bordered in fondant bamboo, handpainted for a realistic
look. The wooden cake board, edged in strips of real bamboo, mimics the shape and look of the cake.*

{NO. 107} *Four tiers of buttercream-frosted cake and three tiers of roses stack up to make a dramatic, romantic confection.*
The flowers—15 to 20 dozen, depending on their size and how open they are—are anchored in a central core of floral foam.
{NO. 108} *The top and bottom sections of this cake display a classic basketweave design, while the thick whorls (made with*
a petal tip) and braided wreaths (a round tip) of the middle tiers copy the artistry of baskets made by Native Americans.

No. 107
TOWER OF
ROSES CAKE

No. 108
RUSTIC
BASKETWEAVE CAKE

SCALLOPED BANDS AND BOWS CAKE

SERVES 150

You can use any type of ribbon on this cake; we used ½-inch-wide center-stitched grosgrain for the bands, and 7-millimeter-wide silk ribbon for the bows.

2 each 7¾ by 5⅝-inch, 10¾ by 7⅝-inch, 13 by 9⅞-inch,
and 16½ by 12⅜-inch oval layers of Marble Cake (recipe follows)

4 pieces corresponding-size ³⁄₁₆-inch-thick foam board

2 batches Swiss Meringue Buttercream (page 238)

Cornstarch, for dusting

12 pounds rolled fondant

Gel-paste food coloring in pink and brown

1 oval cake board (20 by 15½ inches)

28 wooden dowels (¼ inch in diameter, 4⅛ inches long)

Unsweetened cocoa powder, for dusting

Modeling Chocolate

½ batch Royal Icing (page 243)

14 feet ½-inch-wide ribbon, for bands

13 feet 7-millimeter-wide ribbon, for bows

Caramel Sauce (page 244)

1. Prepare the tiers: Trim the layers. On corresponding-size foam boards, fill the layers with buttercream to create 4-inch-tall tiers. Thinly coat with buttercream to seal in the crumbs. Refrigerate for at least 1 hour and up to 1 day.

2. Cover the tiers: On a clean work surface lightly dusted with cornstarch, roll out the fondant (see note below for amounts) for one tier at a time into a small disk. Dip the end of a toothpick into pink food coloring, and press into the fondant. Repeat to create a random pattern of pink marks on the fondant. Fold the edges toward the center; knead 3 or 4 turns. Roll out the fondant until ⅛ inch thick and large enough to cover the largest tier (marbling will be visible). Drape the fondant over a rolling pin; center and place it on the tier. Starting at the top, smooth the fondant onto the cake with your hands. Cut away excess with a pastry wheel. Repeat to cover the remaining tiers. (continued on page 198)

{NO.109} *Marbleized fondant hints at the cake's interior and covers a layer of buttercream frosting. Inside are actually two kinds of cake, chocolate marble and mocha marble, in alternating layers. Once the cake is cut, slices are served to guests in pools of caramel sauce.*

3. Center and place the largest tier on the cake board. Insert 12 dowels, 10 in an oval 2½ inches from the edge and 2 evenly spaced in the center. Center and place the 13-inch tier on top. Insert 10 dowels, 8 about 2½ inches from the edge and 2 evenly spaced in the center. Center and place the 10¾-inch tier on top. Insert the remaining 6 dowels in an oval about 2½ inches from the edge. Top with the 7¾-inch tier.

4. On a work surface dusted with cocoa powder, knead the modeling chocolate until pliable. For each tier, roll a band 2½ inches wide and long enough to go halfway around the tier. Using a pizza cutter, trim the bottom edge to be straight. Trim the top edge with a scallop cutter to make a band 1½ inches high at the scallops' peaks (scraps can be reused). Use a damp pastry brush to moisten the bottom edge of a tier. Working quickly and carefully, lift the band and attach it to the side of the tier, placing the cut ends at the sides of the cake. Repeat with more chocolate to make a band for the other side. To make the band for the cake board, roll out another long band, and trim to about ¾ inch wide. Cut away the top edge using the scallop cutter. Use the damp pastry brush to moisten the area where the cake board meets the edge of the bottom tier. Working quickly, lift the prepared band and press it onto the cake board.

5. Tint ½ cup royal icing brown; transfer to a pastry bag fitted with a coupler and an Ateco #3 round tip. Pipe dots about ½ inch apart around the tiers' bottom edges. Use icing to attach ribbon to the chocolate bands, and bows to the ribbon.

6. To serve, spoon sauce onto a plate; top with a slice of cake.

Approximate fondant amounts (12 pounds total): 7¾-inch tier, 2 pounds; 10¾-inch tier, 2½ pounds; 13-inch tier, 3½ pounds; 16½-inch tier, 4 pounds

MARBLE CAKE
MAKES 13 CUPS BATTER

For approximate batter amounts and baking times for pans, see note below. You will need to bake two of each size pan for each tier. To make tiers of alternating flavors, fill two pans of the same size with chocolate-swirled batter, and two of the other size with mocha-swirled batter. Split cakes in half horizontally, and trim the layers to be 1½ inches thick.

5¼ cups cake flour (not self-rising), plus more for the pans

2 tablespoons baking powder

1½ teaspoons salt

1½ cups (3 sticks) unsalted butter, at room temperature, plus more for the pan

3 cups plus 3 tablespoons sugar

9 large eggs, at room temperature

1 tablespoon pure vanilla extract

2 cups buttermilk, at room temperature

½ cup plus 1 tablespoon best-quality unsweetened cocoa powder (plus 6 tablespoons instant espresso powder, for mocha layers)

¾ cup boiling water

---

1. Preheat the oven to 350°F. Sift together the flour, baking powder, and salt; set aside. Lightly butter the cake pans. Line with parchment paper; butter parchment, and dust with flour, tapping out any excess. Set aside.

2. In the bowl of an electric mixer fitted with the paddle attachment, cream the butter and 3 cups of sugar until light and fluffy, about 5 minutes. Add the eggs one at a time, mixing until incorporated after each. Stir in the vanilla extract.

3. Add the flour mixture in two batches, alternating with the buttermilk, and starting and ending with the flour. Set aside one third of the batter. Combine the cocoa (and espresso powder, if using), remaining sugar, and the boiling water in a small heat-proof bowl; using a rubber spatula, stir until smooth. Stir into the reserved batter.

4. Fill the pans: Use two thirds vanilla and one third chocolate (or mocha) batter, adding batter in large spoonfuls in a checkerboard pattern. Run a wooden skewer lightly through the batter to create a marbled effect.

5. Bake until a cake tester inserted into the centers comes out clean. Transfer to wire racks; cool for 5 minutes. Invert the cakes onto the racks; remove parchment and let cool for 30 minutes.

Approximate batter amounts and baking times for 2-inch-deep oval pans: 7¾ by 5⅝-inch: 2⅔ cups, 35 minutes; 10¾ by 7⅝-inch: 5⅓ cups, 40 minutes; 13 by 9⅞-inch: 8 cups, 45 minutes; 16½ by 12⅜-inch: 12 cups, 50 minutes

Mocha Marble

Chocolate Marble

{NO. IIO} *Stacked mini brownie cakes can replace a wedding cake or be part of the dessert buffet. To make them, bake brownies in a sheet pan and then cut out rounds using graduated round cutters. Set on mismatched china, they are decorated with royal icing, sanding sugar, grated coconut, and confectioners' sugar. Inside-out cupcake liners serve as doilies.*
{NO. III} *White-chocolate fondant encases a grand cake wrapped in marbled bands as well as silk moiré ribbons. The marbling was fashioned using plastic transfer sheets spread with tempered chocolate. (See page 229 for the how-to.)*

No. 110
RICH BROWNIE
CAKES

No. 111
MARBLEIZED
CAKE

making a wedding cake

PLANNING TIPS
204

CAKE 101
212

HELPFUL HOW-TOS
214

{MERINGUE BOUQUET CAKE} *Crisp meringue flowers in varying shades of white encrust this fanciful cake. You can cut right through the blooms to serve the cake—they add a delicious, sweet crunch to each slice.*

Always a meaningful symbol, the wedding cake takes on even greater sentiment when crafted by a friend or a relative (or by the bride or groom). Despite the imposing image of a multitiered construction, the process can be manageable for anyone with basic baking skills and the right equipment.

PLANNING TIPS

IT'S CRUCIAL TO PLAN EARLY AND WISELY. EVEN VET-eran bakers wouldn't dare wait until the last minute to start preparation. You need time to decide on the design and the flavor, to locate any special tools or materials, and to actually create the components. You may also need time to practice particular decorating techniques. Doing a complete dry run long before the wedding day, especially for more complicated constructions, is also a must.

Start by listing all of the necessary tools and materials you will need, including any structural supports and trans-port needs. Then estimate the time it will take to complete everything, from start to finish. Think about what can be made ahead of time, such as cake layers and decorations, and elements that require last-minute attention. Don't agree to do something unless you feel confident in your ability to achieve the desired result. A simple cake that is well executed will be much more impressive than a complex one that looks messy. A visit to the reception site is essential, not only to see how the cake can be displayed, but what the facilities are like for doing any last-minute assembly. Find out if there is a kitchen on-site. If not, is there some other workspace, preferably out of the way and air-conditioned? Also, be sure to check the policy regard-ing cakes made off-site.

If you plan to make separate cakes for serving and display, confirm that there is proper storage space. Check the cake table to make sure it is level (surprisingly, this is not always the case, and it pays to be prepared). In terms of serving sizes, a general rule is to allow a 1- to 2-inch slice per person, depending on the height of the tiers and the richness of the cake.

{FORMING FONDANT} *Martha smooths a thin layer of rolled fondant onto a cake tier. Cornstarch-dusted hands make this step easier. (See page 214 for fondant how-to.)*

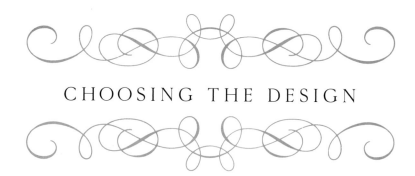

CHOOSING THE DESIGN

- CHOOSE DECORATIONS WISELY. Many embellishments, such as gum-paste or crystallized flowers, marzipan shapes, and stencils or templates, can be purchased from a cake decorator or a specialty store. If you plan to work with chocolate, consider coating chocolate (also called compound chocolate), which does not require tempering and is thus easier to use. It might be a good idea to avoid chocolate altogether for the embellishments, since it is highly sensitive to heat and humidity and can prove difficult to work with under the best of conditions. Other items, such as store-bought candies, truffles, and other confections, can also be used to adorn a cake, especially when their flavors complement the cake. Instead of fresh flowers, which require last-minute attention, use those replicated in gum paste or meringue.

- SELECT ICINGS THAT CAN BE PURCHASED OR MADE AHEAD OF TIME. Fondant is readily available, and chocolate modeling dough is easily made; each has a shelf life of a few months. Buttercream holds up well for several days in the refrigerator or up to a month in the freezer; store it in a tightly sealed container, and allow it to come to room temperature before beating until smooth again (this may take some time, and the frosting will appear curdled, but just keep beating; if necessary, heat it in the microwave for a few seconds and continue beating). For best results, do not tint buttercream until you are ready to use it.

- PICK THE RIGHT MATERIALS FOR THE PARTICULAR EVENT. For example, if you want a way to keep the cake fresh without having to rely on refrigeration, cover it with fondant or marzipan. Buttercream cakes always need to be chilled. Some fillings, too, must be kept chilled. Consult our glossary (page 211) to determine which type of coating or embellishment will work best under certain circumstances, especially hot or humid settings.

- WORK WITH MATERIALS THAT YOU FEEL COMFORTABLE WITH. Fondant requires much practice to perfect, so instead you might want to coat the cake with buttercream or ganache, which are a bit more forgiving. If the reception will be outdoors in the summer, when these and other frostings would melt, you could suggest an uncoated cake, such as a multitiered strawberry shortcake. If you do plan to use fondant, you might want to opt for a firmer cake, such as dacquoise or pound cake, which will be easier to cover smoothly.

- DECIDE ON THE CAKE BASE AT THE OUTSET. This is especially important for larger tiers that won't fit on a traditional stand or platter. If you plan to use a cake board, think about having it cut in the same shape as the bottom tier; there are also ways to extend the cake's design motif to conceal or embellish the board, such as with a colorful ribbon or decorative paper, or by coating it with the same tinted icing that covers the cake.

BAKING THE CAKE LAYERS

- **BEFORE GETTING STARTED,** check to make sure you have all the necessary equipment (see page 211). Cake pans should be the size and depth called for in the recipe (most professional bakers use 3-inch-deep pans) and should not be warped or pitted; make sure the larger ones can fit inside your oven, with the door securely closed. Your oven should be properly calibrated, preferably with an oven thermometer. You will also need several cooling racks (and a place to put them) as well as room in the refrigerator for firming up the cake layers once they've cooled.

- **TO HELP KEEP THE CAKES LEVEL AND FREE OF CRACKING,** try kitchen gadgets called baking strips, such as those made by Magi-Cake; you wet them and wrap them around the pan. Then fill the pans to no more than two thirds of their capacity, and firmly tap the filled pans several times on the countertop to eliminate any air bubbles in the batter. Do not bake too many cakes at one time, since proper air circulation will help them cook evenly. Setting them on a wire rack allows the bottoms of the cakes to cool more quickly.

- **MAKE SURE TO COOK THE CAKES AS DIRECTED IN A RECIPE,** watching for visual and textural cues (such as a cake tester inserted in the middle comes out with just a few crumbs clinging to it). Besides not tasting their best, overcooked cakes will have a hard crust and drier crumb, making them difficult to split and frost neatly; undercooked ones will likely sink in the middle as they cool, resulting in uneven layers.

- **MOST TYPES OF CAKES CAN BE FROZEN** without affecting their taste. In fact, many professional bakers freeze the layers at least overnight, as it helps to firm up the crumb and make it easier to level, split, and crumb-coat the layers. Once the cakes have cooled completely on wire racks, wrap them well in plastic and freeze for up to a month; allow them to defrost completely in the refrigerator, still wrapped, before using.

DECORATING AND
ASSEMBLING THE CAKE

- USE A ROTATING CAKE TABLE to crumb-coat and frost the cake tiers. With some practice and a deft touch, you can create a near-flawless surface that will be an ideal canvas for piping flowers or other decorations. A turntable also allows you to pipe borders in one motion around the circumference of the cake, while turning it with your free hand.

- PRACTICE, PRACTICE, PRACTICE. You can perfect your piping skills on parchment paper or on Styrofoam rounds (available at baking supply stores). Some designs, especially those piped with royal icing or meringue, can be piped onto parchment first and then transferred to the cake.

- IF YOU PLAN TO PIPE FLOWERS (or other designs) onto a cake, first lightly sketch them on the surface (whether fondant or frosting) with a skewer or toothpick; then pipe onto the markings. As a general rule, start with the stems (they appear easy, but piping too quickly can cause them to break; too slowly and they will not be straight). Any mistakes can be filled in with more icing; or, if your cake is well chilled, you might be able to gently scrape off the icing (use a small offset spatula) and try again.

- WELL-CHILLED TIERS ARE EASIER TO HANDLE without damaging the icing. If you have to assemble the cake at the reception site, check to see whether there is storage space for refrigerating the tiers. If not, it might be worth exploring other options, such as renting a refrigerator or several large coolers.

- ASSEMBLE THE CAKE ON THE STAND or board that it will be displayed on during the reception. You can secure the bottom tier to the base with frosting to help prevent it from slipping. When using dowels to support the tiers, you will have to cut them to the proper length (see page 212). Be sure to place the dowels evenly around the tier, just far enough from the edge to be covered by the upper tier (for example, in a 10-inch tier, you might arrange 8 dowels in a circle about 2½ inches from the edge, so an 8-inch tier can rest on top of them).

- MAKE EXTRAS OF EVERYTHING—cake, frostings, fillings, and any decorations—just in case. It's amazing how you can right a lopsided cake by patching it with bits of cake, or fill in any holes with extra buttercream. This is true when you are first assembling the cake, as well as after it's been transported to the site. You'll also want to have more decorations than you need for last-minute replacements.

TRANSPORTING THE CAKE

- MAKE SURE THE CAKE TIERS ARE CONSTRUCTED on either corrugated cardboard or foam board. Heavier base tiers should rest on $\frac{1}{4}$- to $\frac{1}{2}$-inch-thick fiberboard or plywood (which will be secured to the cake board or stand).

- DIRECTLY STACKED CAKES (with tiers that rest on top of each other, without any separators such as pillars) can be transported after being assembled. But if they are particularly wide or have more than two or three tiers, it is better to assemble them at the site. Cakes with supports always need to be assembled at the site.

- BOXES ARE THE SAFEST WAY TO TRANSPORT THE TIERS. Place the tiers (or assembled cake) in clean, covered, heavy-weight boxes; when possible, the box should be just large enough to hold the cake board, as this will prevent the cake from shifting during travel and crushing the sides or any decorations. If the box is too large, place a large nonslip mat on the bottom before setting the cake inside. If your cake is too tall for the box to be closed on top, prop up the sides, secure them with masking tape, and cover the top with plastic wrap.

- YOU WILL NEED A ROOMY, LEVEL SURFACE in the car for the cake boxes; never place them on a seat. Lay a piece of carpet foam or other nonskid mat on the surface, then place the boxes on top. For extra cushioning, you can place a soft blanket on the mat, then layer another mat on top before placing the boxes. If the cake is too large to fit in a box, you can set it directly on the foam or mat (and drive very carefully!).

- IF THE WEATHER IS WARM OR HUMID, be sure to cool the vehicle by running the air-conditioning before placing the cake inside. And remember that air-conditioning never reaches a trunk.

- WHILE THE CAKE IS IN TRANSIT, keep it away from direct sunlight. This is especially important when you have to drive for a lengthy distance or when the cake is too large to be enclosed in a box.

- ONCE YOU'RE AT THE SITE, you may want to have a rolling cart for moving the cake boxes (which may be too heavy to carry) from the car to the display table. This will minimize shifting or the risk of mishaps when carried by hand. Remove the cakes from the boxes by cutting the sides of the boxes and sliding out the cake, rather than trying to lift out the cake from the top.

- ALWAYS PACK A REPAIR KIT with all the necessary decorating tools and materials, including extra frostings and embellishments, and take it with you to the reception site.

EQUIPMENT GLOSSARY

In addition to the items here, you will need a heavy-duty standing mixer, cake pans, parchment paper, cooling racks, and an oven ther-mometer. A nonstick baking mat, such as Silpat, provides a smooth, slick surface for rolling out fondant and other sugar doughs.

{NO. 1} LONG SERRATED KNIFE

This is the knife to use when leveling and splitting cake layers without tearing or crushing. The longer the better for cutting through any size cake layers.

{NO. 2, NO. 3} ROLLING PINS

Smooth wooden ones, with no handles, are best for rolling out fondant, gum paste, chocolate modeling dough, and pastillage.

{NO. 4} PASTRY BRUSHES

Larger ones are ideal for brushing cake layers with syrup, and for sweeping away crumbs from the tops of the layers before filling or frosting.

{NO. 5} PASTRY BAGS AND TIPS

Reusable bags, made of nylon or polyester, are lightweight and comfortable to use. Bags that aren't too large (12 to 16 inches) are best. Tips (also called tubes) are available individually or in sets; sets come with flower nails and a plastic coupler.

{NO. 6, NO. 7} FLORAL SUPPLIES

You will need floral tape and wire, as well as floral foam (not shown), for arrangements that will adorn a cake. These are also used when creating flowers from gum paste.

{NO. 8–NO. 12} GUM-PASTE TOOLS

There are cutters for most flower shapes, veiners for leaves and petals, molds for shaping and making impressions, ball tools and frillers for shaping the edges, plus fine brushes for painting with powdered dusts. A foam square provides the ideal work surface.

{NO. 13} ROTATING CAKE TABLE

When splitting the layers, frosting the tiers, or piping decora-tions, a turntable will make the job much easier, allowing you to rotate the cake smoothly while you work.

{NO. 14} BENCH SCRAPERS

Their straight edges are perfect for crumb-coating and creating smooth sides on buttercream-covered cakes. The model shown here doubles as a ruler, helpful when splitting the layers evenly or piping uniformly spaced details on the cake tiers.

{NO. 15} PIZZA CUTTER

This is the easiest tool to use for cutting fondant, marzipan, and pastillage, especially when trimming the excess from cake tiers.

{NO. 16} GEL-PASTE FOOD COLORS

These concentrated gels are ideal for tinting buttercream and royal icing without watering them down. They can also be used with fondant, gum paste, and marzipan.

{NO. 17} CAKE ROUNDS

Corrugated cardboard rounds (or other precut shapes) are useful for supporting individual cake layers as you work.

{NO. 18} DUSTING POWDERS

Petal dusts can be brushed onto sugar flowers to create realistic dimensions; when mixed with liquid (either oil-based or alcohol), the color is intensified, perfect for painting or highlighting.

{NO. 19} SILICONE SPATULA

This flexible spatula is just right for mixing colors into icings.

{NO. 20} FLOWER FORMERS

These tubes are used to provide curved surfaces for drying icing and chocolate leaves and flower petals for a more natural shape.

{NO. 21} WOODEN DOWELS

Dowels are essential for supporting multitiered cakes. Plastic straws, cut to size, can be used to support smaller cakes.

{NO. 22} METAL SPATULAS

Have at least one large offset spatula for frosting the top, and a smaller one for frosting the sides.

CAKE 101

HOW TO MAKE A BASIC BUTTERCREAM CAKE

1. Each cake tier (these are made from two cake layers, each split, for a total of four layers) needs a sturdy base. Trace around the edge of each cake pan onto a piece of $\frac{3}{16}$-inch-thick foam board (available at art-supply stores). Cut out the rounds using a utility knife with a new blade. Bake cakes in parchment-lined cake pans, and let them cool slightly. Remove from pans. Once completely cool, place each cake right side up on a cardboard round for easy handling, wrap in plastic, and refrigerate for at least 6 hours; this makes the layers firm and easy to handle. They can also be frozen at this point.

2. When ready to assemble the cake, place a dollop of buttercream on the prepared foam board. Place one of the cake layers, bottom side down, on the foam board.

3. Level both cake layers with a serrated knife. Use a turntable to make them even all around. Then split the cake: Hold the serrated knife against the edge of the cake; rotate the turntable, working the knife through the cake. (Once both layers are split, return the one on the foam board to the turntable.)

4. Lift off the top half of this layer; set aside. Brush the bottom layer on the turntable with simple syrup.

5. Spread this layer with filling, about $\frac{1}{4}$ inch thick and extending to the edge. Return the top half of this layer, top side up, and very gently press onto the filling.

6. Continue stacking layers, brushing with syrup before spreading with filling. Place the final layer bottom side up; brush with syrup and let soak 1 to 2 minutes.

7. Generously frost the sides and top with buttercream to give the tier a crumb coat (seal the cake). Start from the center and work out, making sure to push the icing over the sides.

8. Remove the excess buttercream from the sides with a bench scraper; smooth the top edge with an offset spatula. Refrigerate at least 1 hour then apply a final coating of buttercream. Refrigerate again for at least 1 hour.

9. Prepare the cake board at least 8 hours before assembling the cake. The board should be wider (usually 3 to 4 inches) than the bottom tier. You can paint the board, or spread it with thinned royal icing; it's not necessary to ice the center, but the icing must be brought to the edge of the board. Let the royal icing dry completely, at least 8 hours. To build the cake: Place a nonskid mat (or a dollop of buttercream or some hot glue) on the prepared board. Remove the bottom tier from the refrigerator and place it on the board.

10. To trim the dowels, insert a $\frac{1}{4}$-inch dowel vertically into the bottom tier of the cake; mark it flush with the top of the tier (unless you are making floating tiers, in which case you would let the dowels extend slightly above the tiers). Remove it, and cut 8 dowel pieces to this length. These will be the supports for the next tier. Insert 5 cut dowels to form a circle about $1\frac{1}{2}$ inches from the edge of the tier that will be placed on top; arrange the other 3 in a triangle inside the circle.

11. Remove the next tier from the refrigerator. Place about $\frac{1}{2}$ teaspoon of royal icing on top of each dowel. Center and place the next tier on top. Repeat the dowel-and-stacking process for the remaining tiers (except for the top tier), using fewer dowels as the tiers get smaller. Once all tiers are stacked, cut a dowel $\frac{1}{4}$ inch shorter than the height of the assembled cake; to form a pointed tip, cut it with a small pair of branch trimmers (available at hardware stores). Position the point at the center of the top tier; use a mallet to gently drive the dowel down through the center of all the tiers and foam boards. Do not hammer too close to the cake; push in the end with another dowel. Cover the hole with a dab of buttercream; smooth with a small offset spatula. Refrigerate until buttercream is firm.

12. If desired, attach a ribbon to the side of the cake board using double-sided tape. It should be 1 inch larger than the board's circumference and secured in the back.

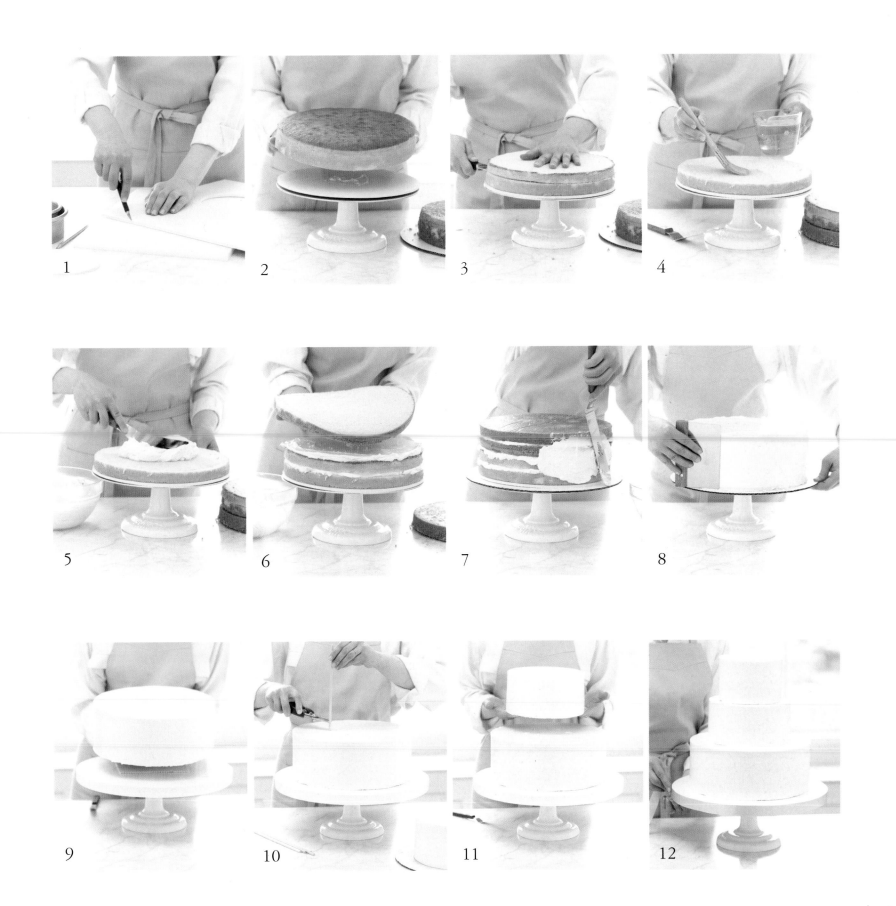

1   2   3   4

5   6   7   8

9   10   11   12

HELPFUL HOW-TOS

In this section, you will find instructions and advice for decorating cakes using versatile ingredients, such as fondant and chocolate, and indispensable tools, such as piping bags and pastry tips. Experiment with these how-tos, and don't hesitate to modify them as you dream up your own ideas. Try making different flowers out of gum paste, for example, or come up with your own piping designs.

WORKING WITH FONDANT

1   2   3   4

COVERING A CAKE

Fondant must be at room temperature before you can use it. Finished tiers or the completed cake can stand at cool room temperature overnight. Because fondant tends to pick up even the tiniest speck of lint, make sure you and your workspace are clean at all times.

---

1. Start by kneading the fondant as you would bread dough. If necessary, dust the work surface very lightly with cornstarch to keep the fondant from sticking. Knead the fondant until it feels soft and pliable. 2. On the same work surface dusted with cornstarch, roll out the fondant to ⅛ inch. If you notice any air bubbles as you roll the fondant, prick them with a clean straight pin. Roll out enough fondant to cover the entire tier you are working on, turning the dough and dusting with more cornstarch as necessary. Excess fondant can be reused for the remaining tiers as long as it has not come into contact with buttercream. 3. Lift the fondant with both hands, and lower it onto the prepared cake tier, working quickly so the fondant doesn't dry out. Dust your hands with cornstarch if necessary, and smooth the top and sides of the cake, pushing out any air bubbles. The fondant will adhere to the buttercream crumb coat. 4. Run a pizza cutter (or a knife) along the edge of the cake, cutting away excess fondant.

IMPRINTING TOOLS

These and other tools can be used to imprint fondant, marzipan, gum paste, and chocolate modeling dough. In most cases, you will not be able to successfully cover a tier with fondant that has already been imprinted; instead, cover the tier with fondant and then make the impressions; some molds and tools create shapes or patterns that are then attached to the iced tier.

{NO. 1} Leaf veiners (see Woodland Nut Cake, page 94) {NO. 2} Eyelet and aspic cutters (see Creamware Cake, page 52, and Eyelet Cake, page 109) {NO. 3} Plastic templates (see Chocolate "Charlotte" Cake, page 172) {NO. 4} Blunt-edged tools (see Garlands and Wreaths Cake, page 104) {NO. 5} Rubber stamps (see Bamboo Wave Cake, page 193, and Homespun Cupcake Tower, page 82) {NO. 6} Perforation wheels (see Silk-Cord Accents Cake, page 128, and Ribbons and Bows Cake, page 181) {NO. 7} Crimper (see Woodland Nut Cake, page 94) {NO. 8} Springerle Molds (see Stately Springerle Cake, page 144)

PIPING 101

1   2   3   4

WORKING WITH PASTRY BAGS

It's a good idea to assemble all of your pastry bags before you get started. When you are ready to pipe, fill the bags with icing and place in tall glasses. If using royal icing, line the glass with a damp paper towel to keep the icing from drying out and clogging the tip.

1. Snip the pointed end of the pastry bag just enough to allow the coupler or the tip to fit inside; use a tip or a coupler to help guide you so you won't cut off too much. (You will need to cut a slightly larger hole for oversize tips.) 2. A coupler allows you to switch among tips to pipe the same frosting. There are two parts: The larger part fits inside the tip of the bag, then the ring screws on from outside the bag, over the tip. To switch tips, simply unscrew the outer ring, and then replace it once the new tip is in place. 3. Take care when filling the bag, as this will make it easier to pipe (and stay neat and clean). Once the tip is in place, twist the bag at the bottom, and then tuck the twisted part inside the tip so that the tip's opening is sealed. Hold the open bag with one hand, folding the top over, and use a spatula (or another piping bag) to fill halfway. Avoid overfilling, as this will make it difficult to keep the frosting from seeping out the top as you work. Close the top of the bag by twisting (or securing with a rubber band). 4. Hold the bag with your writing hand (near the top, so the icing is squeezed down toward the tip) and use your other hand as a guide. Adjust the pressure on the bag depending on the piped design as well as the density of the icing. Buttercream needs gentle pressure; dense royal icing takes stronger pressure. Squeeze the bag as needed as you pipe.

PIPING A MONOGRAM

This technique was used to create the decorations for the Sweeping Monogram Cake on page 54. You can use it to make any design or style of lettering in royal icing.

To make a royal-icing monogram, choose lettering and a monogram style. Create a template, then enlarge to the desired size on a photocopier, making several copies. Place reproductions on a clean, flat surface, cover with waxed paper, and tape in place. Royal icing should not be too thick or too thin (when it is drizzled over the bowl with a spoon, the icing should disappear into the icing in the bowl within 5 to 7 seconds).

To make the letters: Using a #1.5 tip, outline the letters, then flood (or fill in) the outlines. You will need to work quickly before the icing hardens. Once monograms have dried completely, after about 2 hours, gently remove with a thin offset spatula. Make several spares, as letters are fragile. Store letters in an airtight container (up to several weeks). Attach letters to the frosted cake with royal icing.

PIPING GLOSSARY

With a basic set of piping tips (or tubes), a baker can produce hundreds of effects from frosting, depending on the pressure, angle, and flourish applied to the pastry bag. Decorating tips are identified by the "family" they belong to; they are also designated by number, as in the recipes in this book. (We use Ateco tips; other companies may use different numbers.) Nearly every tip comes in a range of sizes for even greater variety. See the following page for examples of each of the below tips. The R O U N D *(or plain) tip is the most versatile; use it like a pen to draw delicate vines, flowers, fleurs-de-lis, and dots (as well as letters). The three* S T A R *tips—open, closed, and French or fine—can be used to pipe stars, rosettes, hearts, peaks, and scallops, either separately or strung together to create beautiful borders. The* P E T A L *tip is essential for piping flowers; this tip is also good for creating ruffles and ribbons. A* B A S K E T W E A V E *tip is right not only for what its name suggests but also for forming pleats and ribbed borders. A* L E A F *tip draws a ribbon with a vein down the middle and is used to pipe foliage of different shapes and sizes. The standard type makes a flat shape, while the* V L E A F *tip produces a more textured design.* O V E R S I Z E *tips, whatever the design, are ideal for fashioning dramatically large effects, such as peaked kisses (see the Meringue Chrysanthemum Cake, page 130).*

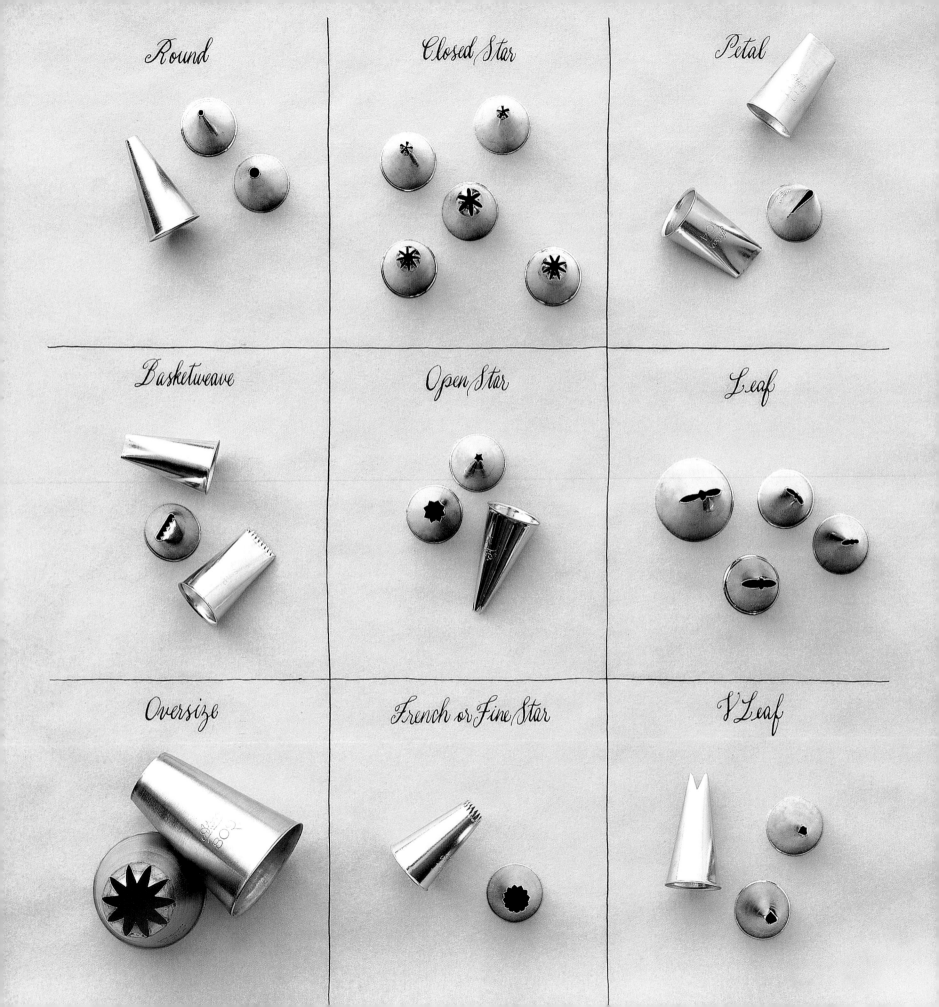

Round

Closed Star

Petal

Basketweave

Open Star

Leaf

Oversize

French or Fine Star

8 Leaf

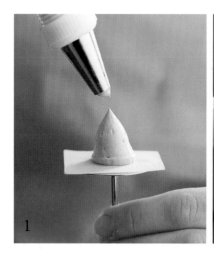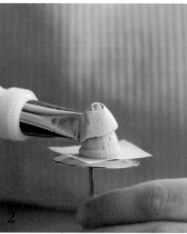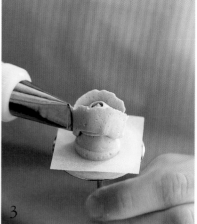

PIPING A ROSE

You'll need a flower nail (we used a #7), available in baking supply stores, to make roses. (When you need both hands to switch tips or colors, anchor the nail in a block of floral foam.) Use a small offset spatula to transfer roses to the top of a cake.

1. Dab frosting on the top of the nail to secure a small square of parchment paper on top. Using the #12 round tip, squeeze the bag gently and pull up slowly to make an acorn shape on top of the parchment. 2. Switch to the #103 petal tip. Holding the tip against the point of the acorn, wide end down and the narrow end angled in toward the acorn's center, pipe a wide strip as you turn the nail, enrobing the top completely. 3. Turning the nail as you go, make two slightly arched petals that each reach around half of the circumference of the acorn. 4. Continue turning the nail, making longer petals that overlap, until you reach the bottom of the rose. Gently slide the parchment with the rose onto a baking sheet; refrigerate for at least 20 minutes.

PIPING BASKETWEAVE PATTERNS

There are many ways to pipe a basketweave pattern with buttercream (see opposite). For example, you can vary the number or color of the lines, or use different tips to create dramatically different results. First practice on parchment paper, then you might want to try your hand covering a Styrofoam tier before tackling a real cake. See pages 63, 177, and 195 for examples of cakes that use this popular effect.

Follow this basic process for making any type of basketweave: First, pipe a vertical line of buttercream (on a cake, this line would cover the entire height of the tier, from top to bottom). Pipe a series of short horizontal lines over the vertical line, extending over by about ½ inch, and leaving about ½ inch between the horizontal lines. Pipe another vertical line to the right of the first, covering the ends of the horizontal lines. In alternate spaces between the first horizontal lines, pipe another set overlapping the second vertical line. Continue until the entire tier is covered. 1. Follow the basic procedure described above, but with different tips. Left: #48 basketweave tip; center: #5 round tip; right: #70 leaf tip. 2. Use different tips to create contrasting vertical and horizontal lines or to add another layer of dimension on top. Left: A #16 star tip for the vertical and #47 basketweave tip (using the flat, or underside, of the tip) for the horizontal. Center: Use a #47 tip for the vertical and a #5 round tip for the horizontal, with two parallel lines for each band. Right: Use a #45 plain (non-serrated) basketweave tip for both directions, and a #102 rose petal tip to pipe the loops on top. 3. You can also vary the color of the lines to vary the pattern. Left: Use a #5 round tip for both vertical and horizontal bands, each one consisting of parallel lines. Center: The plain vertical lines were piped with a #7 round tip, the horizontal lines with the #48 tip. Right: Use a #16 star tip was used to pipe the plain lines in both directions, with alternate pink vertical lines piped with a #4 round tip.

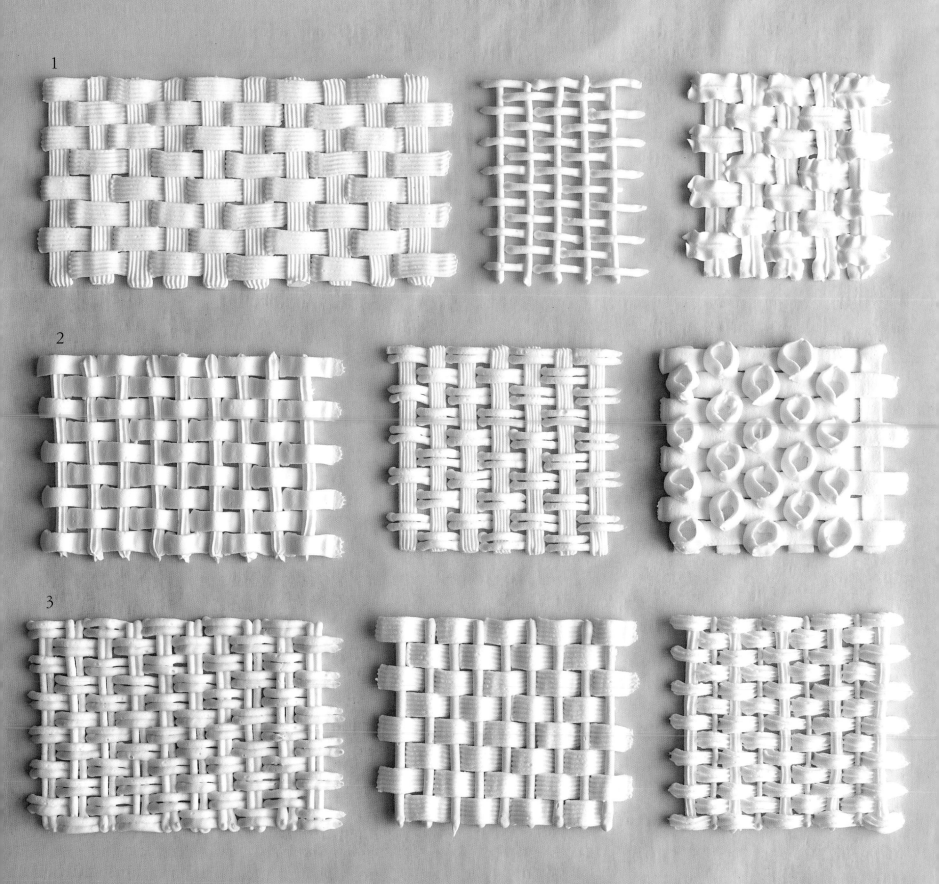

A PIPING GLOSSARY

See pages 48–49 for the Seven-Tier Classic Cake, which features this intricate piping. To create these designs, you will need the following tips: plain round tips (#3, #5), star tips (#14, #16, #22), and small flower tip (#101). The cake tiers are numbered from top to bottom.

FIRST ROW *(middle of second tier):* Mark the center of the tier and measure and mark 1-inch increments around the tier. Using a #5 tip, pipe 1-inch scrolled hearts, moving from left to right, around the tier. Pipe a small pearl trim inside each heart, then pipe a small pearl trim in an elongated "S" pattern on each side of the hearts.

SECOND ROW *(bottom of second tier):* To make the vertical shell with trellis for the base border, use a #16 star tip to pipe upright tapered shells. Use a #2 round tip to pipe trellis loops, overlapping the shells slightly and alternating the loops between each two points of shells. The bottom of the loops should cover the base of each shell.

THIRD ROW *(first tier):* For the upturned scallops at the base of the tier, invert the covered tier onto a clean rotating cake table; working upside down allows gravity to help create perfect upturned scallops. Working quickly, using the #3 tip, pipe scallops around the "top" edge (which is actually the bottom edge, since the tier is upside down), spacing them about 1½ inches apart. Pipe another scallop just above this scallop. Overpipe the first scallop two more times. Wait 2 minutes, then turn the tier right side up. Pipe small dots just above the scallops. For the top edge of the tier: Using the #16 star tip, pipe elongated S scrolls around the edge. Switch to tip #3 round and pipe a 1-inch-wide scallop just below the tight curl of the S scroll. Then pipe another wider scallop just to where the next S scroll begins. Pipe another series of scallops below these scallops. Overpipe the upper scallops two times. Overpipe the lower scallops one time. Just below the upper scallop, using a #2 tip, pipe a small pearl edging.

FOURTH ROW *(third tier):* To make the top shell and scallop border, start by piping shells with a #22 tip, tapering them inward but allowing some space in between. Then, with a #14 star tip, pipe a "question mark" over the shell. Pipe a small scroll at the base of the shell, on the right side. Switch to a #3 tip, and overpipe each scroll and its smaller scroll to the right. With the #14 tip, pipe zigzag scallops above the shells, then overpipe with the same tip, only do not zigzag. Using the #3 tip, pipe three trellis loops below each shell; on the final trellis loop, skip every other point on the previously piped loops.

FIFTH ROW *(sixth tier):* To pipe the crescent scallop pattern, divide the tier into equal sections, marking them with a toothpick. Use a #3 or #5 tip to outline the crescent scallop within each section. Use a #16 tip to pipe the base, tapering it at both ends, then overpipe with the same tip. Use a #101 tip to pipe a serrated edge on the base; use a #16 tip to pipe C scrolls on top. Use a #3 tip to overpipe the entire scallop, including the C scroll. Use a #5 tip to pipe modified fleurs-de-lys between the C scrolls.

SIXTH ROW *(fourth tier):* To pipe the inverted C scroll with shell base, divide the tier into 16 even sections, marking the sections at the bottom of the tier with a toothpick. Using the #22 tip, pipe an upright tapered shell within each section. Use the #16 tip to pipe inverted C scrolls between the shells; then overline each scroll and pipe a three-stroke plume on each shell. Use a #5 tip to pipe roped scallops in the space between shells. Use a #3 tip to pipe fine multi-scalloping above the #5 scallops; then, beneath the #5 scallops, pipe the pulled-pearl scallop. Finish by piping a shell border at the base with the #16 tip.

LAST ROW *(fifth tier):* To pipe the lattice border at the base, first divide the tier into equal sections, marking them at the base; then measure and mark parallel sections for the top scallop border. Use a #3 or #5 tip to outline the scallops at top and bottom. Use a #3 tip to pipe a lattice around the entire cake, first to the right, then to the left. Using #3 and #5 tips, pipe graduated scallops at the top, ending with a fine scallop edge. Use #16 and #5 tips to pipe the scallops at the base. Finish by piping a small dot border around the base with a #3 tip.

WORKING WITH FRESH FLOWERS

BUILDING FLORAL DISPLAYS

When you want to add a floral "tier" (see the Tower of Roses, page 194, and the Demure Beaded Cake, page 116), you need to consider the support, just as you would for a tier made of cake. You also need to protect the other tiers from any water that might drip off. This is the technique Wendy uses. Some bakers use plastic pillars instead of a Styrofoam round to create the height, encasing the pillars in floral foam, such as Oasis. Instead of arranging the flowers at the end, some bakers prefer to arrange most of them in the foam before stacking the tiers, and then fine-tune after the cake is assembled. You should feel free to experiment to come up with your own method.

1. To build a floral tray that will rest on top of a 10-inch tier (and below an 8-inch tier), you will need an 8-inch masonite board, an 8-inch plastic drip tray (its edge trimmed to ½ to 1 inch high), an 8-inch (or 7-inch) plastic separator plate, and a 6-inch-diameter by 4-inch-tall round of floral foam. Arrange a few pieces of floral tape on top of the masonite board, then secure the drip tray in place. Arrange more pieces of tape in the base of the drip tray, and place the floral foam round on top, pressing gently to adhere. Then wrap several strips of the tape around the foam and drip tray, and set the plastic separator plate on top. (Using a level will ensure that the assembled unit is completely even.) 2. Stack the tiers: Insert dowels into a cake tier (see page 212) and place the 8-inch floral tier on top. Place a few pieces of tape on top of the separator plate, then center and place the next cake tier on top. 3. Insert flowers into the floral foam as desired. 4. Be sure that the foam is completely concealed by the flowers.

MAKING CRYSTALLIZED FLOWERS

When coated with superfine sugar, fresh flowers make a beautiful cake decoration. Flowers that work best are those without lots of petals. Small leaves, such as rose or citrus, make lovely accents. Check with your caterer or florist to be sure that the flowers you use are edible.

1. Beat 2 egg whites in a bowl, and mix with 2 tablespoons water. (Or mix the water with powdered egg whites or meringue powder.) Trim the stems off the flowers; dip each blossom into the egg mixture, coating the entire flower. **2.** Lightly shake off any excess, and blot the flower with a paper towel. **3.** Holding the flower above a bowl of superfine sugar, sprinkle sugar over the entire flower with a spoon. Place the sugared flowers on a wire rack (to catch excess sugar, place the rack on a baking sheet), and leave them to dry overnight at room temperature.

USING EDIBLE FLOWERS

Edible flowers, such as roses, hibiscus, snapdragons, nasturtiums, pansies, and calendula, can serve as decorations on the cake and garnishes. It's a good rule of thumb to not put anything on the plate—even as a garnish—that cannot safely be eaten. Flowers that are not edible but are nontoxic can also embellish a cake, but they must be removed before the cake is served. Toxic flowers should be avoided altogether; they can be rendered in gum paste, frosting, or fabric instead.

Some flowers, even edible ones, may trigger allergic reactions, particularly in individuals who suffer from hay fever or asthma. If you decide to use edible flowers, they should be ordered through your florist or specialty dealer; confirm that they are grown without pesticides and, ideally, grown organically. Your caterer or baker should know which flowers are safe and should make sure that the vendor who's providing them knows that they are to be part of the cake.

WORKING WITH GUM PASTE

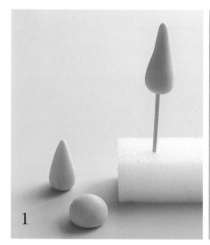  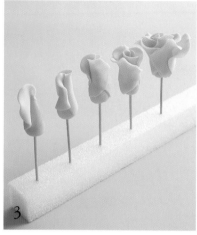 

MAKING A GUM-PASTE ROSE

This technique is for any flower consisting of a bud surrounded by a cluster of petals. To mimic the variations of a real rose, tint gum paste four different shades of the same color. Use the darkest hues to form the center, graduating to the lightest pink for the outermost petals. Here, we tinted it pink, but you could use any natural rose color. Use gel-paste colorings for the best results.

1. Roll a bit of dark-pink paste into a ball, then pinch into a cone. To make it easier to work with, mount the cone on a toothpick inserted into Styrofoam. 2. To make petals, roll the gum paste paper-thin, then cut with petal-shaped cutters of various sizes. Using a ball tool, thin and curl the edges of the petals, giving them a ruffled texture. The smooth foam mat underneath acts as a cushion. 3. Attach the petals one by one around the cone. Wet the edges of the petals with water so they adhere to the cone, or use a liquid gum glue, which forms a stronger bond. The rose must dry thoroughly before being removed from the toothpick. This can take a few days in a humid climate, less time in a drier one. 4. The finished rose can have any number of petals. This fully opened blossom has twelve; a bud might have only six.

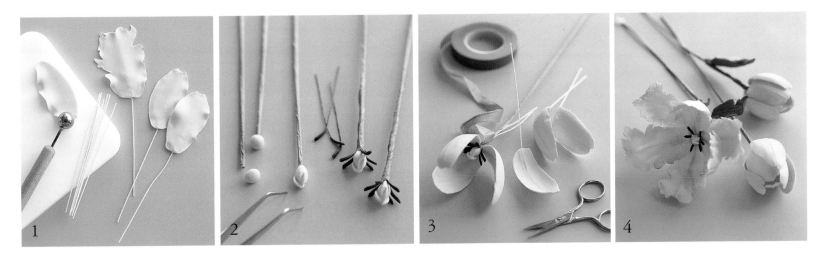

MAKING A GUM-PASTE TULIP

Most tulips have six petals. Since they are formed with floral tape and wire, the tulips should be removed before the cake is served.

1. Tint the gum paste, then roll it out thin and cut into petals. Use a cutter with smooth sides to form basic tulips, or an irregularly shaped one to create ruffled edges for parrot tulips. Using a ball tool, thin the petals' edges; thread onto wires. Press the cutouts into a silicone mold. Let the petals dry in plastic molds. 2. For the centers, push a ball of gum paste onto a wire wrapped in floral tape. Use tweezers to pinch it into a natural shape. Place the stamens around the center and affix to the stem with floral tape. 3. Once dry, attach the petals by taping their wires to the stem. Brush with several shades of yellow petal dust. 4. The parrot tulip is shown open. The others are more closed, as if they have just come into bloom.

MAKING GUM-PASTE CHERRY BLOSSOMS

This technique can be adapted for many other flowers with five or six petals. To give the cake a more natural look, make some individual petals as well. (See the Pink Cherry Blossom Cake, page 112, which uses this technique.)

1. Roll the gum paste paper-thin, then cut with rounded petal-shaped cutters in graduated sizes. 2. Using a ball tool, thin and curl the petal edges, giving them a slightly ruffled texture. 3. Tint dried blossoms with petal dusts, using a soft-bristled brush.

WORKING WITH MARZIPAN

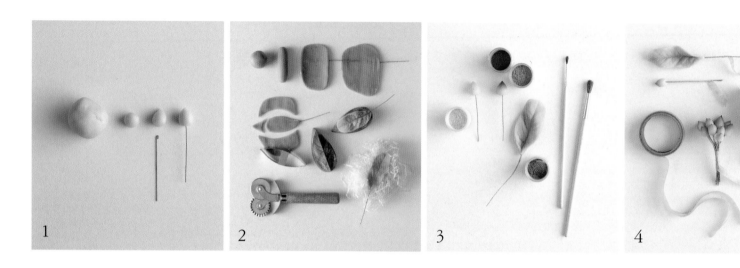

MAKING MARZIPAN NUTS AND LEAVES

This how-to is for the clusters of pistachios and leaves on the Woodland Nut Cake (page 95), but the techniques can be easily adapted for creating other marzipan decorations. Using gel-paste food coloring, tint marzipan in desired shades. To tint: Use a toothpick or a skewer to add food coloring, a little at a time, to the marzipan, then knead until the color is uniform. Avoid adding too much color to the marzipan too soon; the intensity will increase with continued kneading.

1. To make the pistachios, mold small pieces of marzipan into nut shapes. Insert wires into the shapes. 2. To make the leaves, roll green-tinted marzipan into a log; roll the log out horizontally so one side is thicker and the other side is ⅛ inch thick. Slightly dampen a 4-inch-long, 22-gauge floral wire with water or gum glue. Insert wire into the thick side of the log, about 1 inch deep. Further thin the marzipan by rolling from the wire to the edge. Cut with leaf cutters, and press large leaves in a leaf veiner. 3. If desired, brush the pistachios with petal dust (in colors such as Buttercup, Burgundy, and Old Rose) or cocoa powder to accent with additional color. Green petal dust may be used to add highlights to leaves. 4. To assemble, wrap leaves around the pistachio shapes; tape wires together using green floral tape. Let dry on a paper-towel-lined baking sheet overnight.

WORKING WITH CHOCOLATE

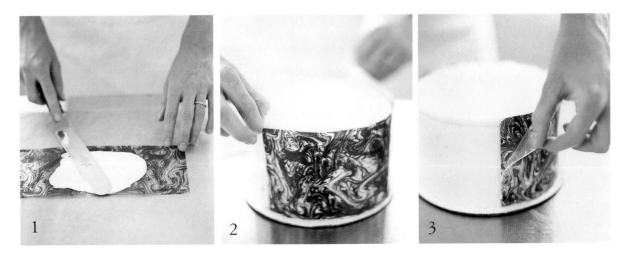

MARBLEIZING WITH TRANSFER SHEETS

Marbleized transfer sheets make decorating cake tiers, as shown on page 201, a snap. Use melted white chocolate to "glue" on the design.

1. Melt white chocolate in a heat-proof bowl set over a pan of simmering water, stirring until smooth. Cut the transfer sheet to the height of the tier (you may need several sheets to go all the way around; cut them to meet exactly without overlap). Spread the sheet with a thin layer of melted white chocolate, smoothing it with a small offset spatula to the corners and edges. Let it stand for a few seconds to thicken slightly. 2. Carefully lift the sheet by the corners, and wrap it around the fondant-covered tier snugly. 3. Let the chocolate set completely before peeling off the plastic. Repeat to cover the entire tier.

TEMPERING CHOCOLATE

When chocolate is tempered—melted and cooled, then warmed to specific temperatures—it will be glossy and break with a "snap" once hardened. If you melt chocolate but do not temper it, the result may be dull and grainy. Always use the best-quality couverture chocolate. The following numbers are for Valrhona; check the package for proper temperatures for your brand. Do not let water droplets get in the bowl (the chocolate will seize, or harden), and to avoid an inaccurate reading, do not allow the thermometer to touch the bottom of the bowl. To temper: 1. Chop chocolate into $\frac{1}{4}$-inch pieces; melt two-thirds in a heat-proof bowl set over a pan of barely simmering water. 2. Stir gently with a rubber spatula until chocolate reaches 118°F on a chocolate thermometer. 3. Remove the bowl from heat; add remaining chocolate. Stir gently with the spatula until the chocolate cools to 84°F. Remove any unmelted pieces and discard. Return the bowl to the pan; stir until the chocolate reaches 84°F to 88°F (for milk chocolate) or 88°F to 90°F (for dark chocolate). Use immediately for piping and molding.

MAKING CHOCOLATE BANDS

These bands were used to decorate the Chocolate "Charlotte" Cake (page 172), but you could use a similar process to create your own designs. Because the chocolate bands are delicate, you will need to make and attach them once the cake is at the final display place.

To create textured chocolate bands, you'll need modeling chocolate, cocoa powder, a straightedge, a pizza cutter, a dry pastry brush, a plastic imprinter, a small rolling pin, and a straight frill cutter. Lightly dust a clean, dry work surface with cocoa. Divide modeling chocolate into pieces; work with one at a time. (Larger tiers will require several bands.) Roll into a 4-inch-wide band, about $\frac{3}{16}$ inch thick; using the straightedge and pizza cutter, cut one long edge to be straight. Brush band lightly with cocoa. Lay plastic imprinter over chocolate; press evenly with rolling pin, working in sections and slightly overlapping pattern; repeat until entire band is crimped. Cutting $3\frac{1}{2}$ inches from straightedge, use frill cutter to scallop other edge. Repeat with all bands. To assemble, position the cake (on board) on the cake table. Carefully transfer chocolate bands to the cake, wrapping each tier and pressing to secure; gently bend frilled edges over tops of tiers. Wrap with a ribbon that's been cut so ends meet without overlapping; tape ends together in center front of cake. Attach premade bow to cover the seam with double-sided tape.

MAKING CHOCOLATE LEAVES

When choosing a leaf—from a nonpoisonous, pesticide-free plant—to use for molding chocolate, avoid varieties with a fuzzy underside that will cling to the chocolate. We found crimson grape leaves released the chocolate most easily; lemon leaves are another good option.

1. Gently clean the leaves with a damp paper towel, and let dry completely. Paint a thin layer of tempered chocolate (see page 229) on the underside of each leaf (here we used white chocolate). Refrigerate until set, 2 to 3 minutes. Paint on another layer of chocolate, and chill again; repeat until leaves are coated with four layers of chocolate. 2. Once chocolate is completely set, snip off the stem. Slide the tip of a paring knife between the leaf and chocolate, and peel off the leaf. Lightly dust the tops of the dry, cool leaves with cocoa powder; remove any excess with a clean, dry brush. Store finished leaves in a cool, dry spot.

MAKING CHOCOLATE WOOD GRAIN (FAUX BOIS)

To create a wood-grain effect, as on the cake on page 125, you will need one strip of acetate for each side of each tier, cut to the same size. The wood-grain tool should be wider than the trimmed acetate strips. You will need 12 ounces of white chocolate and 2 pounds of bittersweet chocolate to cover a cake with four 5-inch-high tiers (15, 12, 9, and 6 inches square).

1. Cut a large piece of thin acetate into strips that are as tall and as long as one side of each of the tiers. Place strips on a clean work surface with short sides facing you. Coat the surface of a wood-graining tool (available at paint supply stores, or see Sources, page 254) with a thick layer of melted white chocolate. Starting at the top of an acetate strip, rock the coated tool back and forth while dragging it in one swift motion to make a vertical striation. Transfer the acetate, chocolate side up, to an upside-down rimmed baking sheet; refrigerate until set, about 6 minutes. 2. Temper bittersweet chocolate (see page 229). Immediately pour the tempered chocolate on top of the coated acetate. Using an offset spatula, quickly but gently spread evenly over the entire surface (do not spread it too much or the white chocolate will smear). Gently press the acetate, chocolate side down, onto the frosted tiers. Refrigerate until the wood grain is hardened, at least 1 hour. 3. Carefully peel off the acetate just before displaying the cake.

ADDITIONAL TECHNIQUES

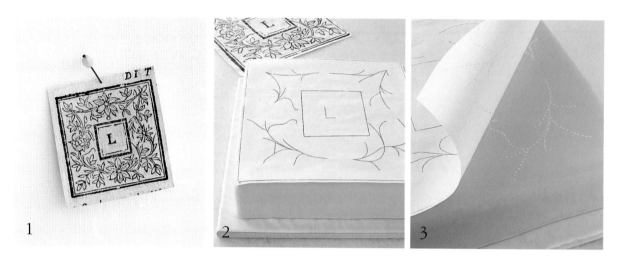

TRANSFERRING A MONOGRAM DESIGN

Letters found in vintage books or print shops can inspire beautiful cakes. If you find a monogram that you would like to use as a cake decoration, you can take the following steps to transfer the design from paper to a fondant-covered tier (see page 189).

---

1. Reduce or enlarge the design on a photocopy machine until it fills the area of the tier you would like to decorate. **2.** Using straight pins, secure the photocopied design to the fondant-covered cake tier in areas where the pinholes will not be noticed. Using another straight pin, prick holes through the design's outlines into the fondant, keeping the holes about ¼ inch apart. On our blue "L" cake we transferred only the main contours of the letter and the surrounding leaves and vines (and then filled in the finer details directly onto the fondant after the paper was removed). **3.** Remove the pins securing the paper, then carefully lift off the paper. When applying the leaves and vines, refer back to the original picture to determine the precise placement of each.

MAKING MERINGUE MUSHROOMS

These mushrooms were used to decorate the cake on page 101. For the recipe and detailed instructions, see page 246.

1. Pipe meringue into the shape of mushroom caps and stems, then bake as directed. 2. Spread melted bittersweet chocolate onto undersides of caps; when set, top with a layer of white chocolate. 3. Use a toothpick to gently carve lines in the white chocolate to create the gills. Then carve holes in the centers. 4. Attach the stems using more melted white chocolate.

MAKING ICING DAMASK

We borrowed this design from a favorite swatch of fabric to decorate the Damask Cake (page 187), but you could use anything as inspiration. To create the template, we first scanned a sketched image onto a computer so that it could be printed in duplicate; if you prefer, trace a design onto paper. Piped decorations are very fragile, so always make extras, at least two more per tier.

1. Place the pattern under wax paper. 2. Using dark-brown royal icing, pipe the outline; fill in with thinned royal icing (called floodwork). 3. After it dries, lift the hardened icing with an artist's palette knife (do not use an offset spatula). 4. Pipe thick royal icing, also tinted dark brown, onto the back of the design, then carefully affix it to the cake.

Use the chart on page 252 to determine the batter amounts and baking times for four common tier sizes.

ALMOND-CORNMEAL POUND CAKE

MAKES 11 CUPS BATTER

Cornmeal replaces some of the flour in this recipe, resulting in a cake with a bit more heft and a distinctive texture. This cake would be lovely with Mascarpone Cream Filling (page 243).

1 pound (4 sticks) unsalted butter, very soft,
plus more for the pans

5¼ cups cake flour (not self-rising), sifted,
plus more for the pans

13 ounces almond paste

2⅔ cups sugar, plus ¼ cup and 2 tablespoons sugar
for the egg whites

2⅔ cups milk

2 teaspoons pure vanilla extract

16 large eggs, at room temperature, separated

2 cups stone-ground yellow cornmeal

4 teaspoons baking powder

1 teaspoon salt

1. Preheat the oven to 350°F, with a rack in the lower third. Brush the cake pans (see chart, page 252) with butter. Line each with parchment paper; butter parchment, and dust with flour, tapping out any excess. Set aside. Put the almond paste and 2⅔ cups sugar in a food processor; process until very fine.

2. Transfer the mixture to the bowl of an electric mixer fitted with the paddle attachment. Add the butter; mix on medium speed until soft and pale, about 4 minutes.

3. Meanwhile, whisk together the milk, vanilla, and egg yolks in a medium bowl. In a separate bowl, whisk together the flour, cornmeal, baking powder, and salt. With the mixer running, gradually add the flour mixture and milk mixture in alternating additions, beginning and ending with the flour; mix until combined.

4. In the clean bowl of an electric mixer fitted with the whisk attachment, beat the egg whites until foamy, then gradually add the remaining ¼ cup and 2 tablespoons sugar on medium speed and beat until medium stiff peaks form, 2 to 3 minutes. Fold one third of the whites into the batter to lighten, then fold in the remaining whites in two batches.

5. Pour the batter into the prepared pans, filling each two-thirds full. Bake until golden and a cake tester inserted into the centers comes out clean (if the top browns too quickly, tent with foil during the last 15 to 20 minutes of baking). Let cool completely in pans on wire racks.

WHITE BUTTER CAKE
MAKES 6 CUPS BATTER

This versatile cake is best baked the day before it
will be served (wrap well and refrigerate). To add moisture
and flavor, brush the layers with simple syrup.

*14 tablespoons (1¾ sticks) unsalted butter,
at room temperature, plus more for the pans*

*3¼ cups sifted cake flour (not self-rising),
plus more for dusting*

1½ tablespoons baking powder

¼ teaspoon salt

1 cup plus 2 tablespoons milk

1 tablespoon pure vanilla extract

1¾ cups sugar

5 large egg whites, at room temperature

1. Preheat the oven to 350°F. Brush the cake pans (see chart,
page 252) with butter. Line with parchment paper; butter parchment, and dust with flour, tapping out any excess. Set aside.

2. Whisk together the flour, baking powder, and salt into a
medium bowl; set aside. Stir the milk and vanilla to combine;
set aside. In the bowl of an electric mixer fitted with the paddle
attachment, cream butter until pale and fluffy, about 3 minutes. Add the sugar in a steady stream; mix until pale and
fluffy, about 3 minutes.

3. Reduce the speed to low. Add the flour mixture in three
additions, alternating with the milk mixture, and beginning
and ending with the flour; mix just until combined.

4. In a clean mixing bowl, whisk the egg whites just until stiff
peaks form. Fold one third of the egg whites into the batter to
lighten. Gently fold in the remaining whites in two batches.
Divide the batter among the prepared pans; smooth the tops
with an offset spatula. Firmly tap the pans on a work surface
to release any air bubbles.

5. Bake until a cake tester inserted into the centers comes out
clean and the tops are springy to the touch. Let cool in the
pans on wire racks for 15 minutes. Invert the cakes onto the
racks. Remove the parchment; reinvert and cool completely.

APPLE CAKE
MAKES ABOUT 8 CUPS BATTER

This autumnal cake is wonderfully moist and
will keep well for several days; wrap well and refrigerate.
Pair the cake with Caramel–Cream Cheese Filling
(page 243) and Caramel Buttercream (page 239).

*1½ cups (3 sticks) unsalted butter, at room temperature,
plus more for the pans*

2¼ cups all-purpose flour

2¼ teaspoons baking soda

2 teaspoons ground cinnamon

1 teaspoon salt

*3 medium apples (preferably Granny Smith),
cored and peeled*

1 cup granulated sugar

1 cup dark brown sugar

3 large eggs

2 teaspoons pure vanilla extract

1 cup apple butter

2 tablespoons vegetable oil

1. Preheat the oven to 350°F. Coat the cake pans (see chart,
page 252) with butter; line the bottoms with parchment paper,
and coat parchment. Set aside. Sift together the flour, baking
soda, cinnamon, and salt into a large bowl. Shred the apples on
a box grater. Transfer to paper towels; press firmly to drain. In
a bowl, toss with ½ cup of the flour mixture to coat.

2. Mix the butter and sugars in an electric mixer fitted with
the paddle attachment until fluffy. Add the eggs, one at a time,
mixing well after each. Add the remaining flour mixture; mix
to combine. Mix in the vanilla, apple butter, and oil, then mix
in the shredded apples. Divide the batter among pans.

3. Bake until a cake tester inserted into the centers comes out
clean. Let cool in pans on wire racks for 15 minutes. Invert the
cakes onto the racks. Remove the parchment; reinvert and cool
completely.

CARROT CAKE
MAKES 13½ CUPS BATTER

The carrots can be peeled and chopped and then shredded in a food processor. This moist cake, redolent with spices, pairs particularly well with Cream Cheese Frosting (page 241) or White Chocolate Buttercream (page 238).

Vegetable-oil cooking spray

6 cups all-purpose flour, plus more for the pans

2 pounds carrots, peeled and finely grated

6 large eggs, at room temperature

⅔ cup nonfat buttermilk, at room temperature

4 cups sugar

3 cups vegetable oil

*2 vanilla beans, halved lengthwise,
seeds scraped and reserved*

1 cup golden raisins

4 teaspoons baking powder

2 teaspoons baking soda

2 teaspoons salt

2 teaspoons ground cinnamon

2 teaspoons ground ginger

¼ teaspoon ground cloves

1. Preheat the oven to 325°F. Coat the cake pans (see chart, page 252) with cooking spray. Line with parchment; dust with flour, and tap out any excess. Set aside.

2. Whisk together the carrots, eggs, buttermilk, sugar, oil, vanilla seeds, and raisins in a large bowl. Whisk together the flour, baking powder, baking soda, salt, cinnamon, ginger, and cloves in a medium bowl. Stir the flour mixture into the carrot mixture until completely combined. Transfer the batter to the prepared pans.

3. Bake until a cake tester inserted in the centers comes out clean. Transfer to wire racks; let cool in the pans for 40 minutes. Unmold onto racks. Remove the parchment and cool completely.

ALMOND DACQUOISE
MAKES 7 CUPS BATTER

Dacquoise is essentially a meringue with the addition of lots of nuts. It can be made several days in advance; wrap well with plastic and store in a cool, dry place.

Vegetable-oil cooking spray

All-purpose flour, for the pans

2 cups finely ground blanched almonds

1 cup superfine sugar

1½ cups confectioners' sugar

8 large egg whites

1. Preheat the oven to 200°F. Draw circles on parchment paper (6, 8, 10, or 12 inch, as desired). Spray baking sheets with cooking spray. Turn the parchment over so the drawings are facing down, and place on baking sheets. Set aside.

2. Whisk together the almonds, ½ cup of the superfine sugar, and the confectioners' sugar; set aside. In the bowl of an electric mixer fitted with the whisk attachment, beat the egg whites until they form soft peaks. One tablespoon at a time, slowly add the remaining ½ cup superfine sugar; continue to beat until the mixture forms stiff peaks. Fold in the nut mixture. Spread the mixture inside the circles on the prepared baking sheets to a thickness of ¼ inch.

3. Bake the dacquoise for 2 hours; then turn off the oven, and leave inside until completely cooled, about 30 minutes. Wrap each piece individually in plastic wrap, and set aside until ready to use.

LEMON POPPY SEED POUND CAKE

MAKES ABOUT 19 CUPS BATTER

Poppy seeds give this tangy pound cake
subtle crunch and, when sliced and plated, a delightful
flecked appearance. The batter bakes up very
dark and with a firm crust, so for best results trim the top,
bottom, and sides of the cakes before frosting.

*30 tablespoons (3¾ sticks) unsalted butter,
melted and cooled, plus more for pans*

10 lemons

4½ cups sugar

8¼ cups all-purpose flour

4½ teaspoons baking powder

2¼ cups crème fraîche

18 large eggs

6 tablespoons poppy seeds

1. Preheat the oven to 350°F with the racks in the lower half. Coat the cake pans (see chart, page 252) with butter; line the bottoms with parchment paper, and coat parchment. Dust with flower and tap out any excess. Set aside.

2. Grate the zest of the lemons (you should have about 10 tablespoons). Blend the zest with the sugar in a food processor until fine. Remove the pith from each lemon with a sharp knife. Working with one at a time, hold the lemon over a bowl, and carve out the flesh between the membranes, allowing the segments to drop into the bowl (you should have about 1½ cups segments). Squeeze the juice from the membranes into the bowl; strain the juice (you should have about ⅔ cup). Chop the segments into ½-inch pieces; strain off any juice and toss with ¼ cup of the flour.

3. Sift the remaining 8 cups flour and the baking powder into the bowl of an electric mixer; add the lemon sugar. Attach the bowl to the mixer and fit with the paddle attachment. With the mixer on low speed, add the crème fraîche. Raise the speed to medium. Add the eggs, one at a time, mixing well after each addition. Reduce the speed to low. Gradually add the melted butter and lemon juice; mix until combined. Mix in the poppy seeds; fold in the lemon segments. Divide the batter among the prepared pans.

4. Bake until a skewer inserted into the centers comes out clean. (If the cakes become too dark while baking, cover with foil.) Transfer to wire racks; let cool in the pans slightly. Invert the cakes onto racks. Remove the parchment; reinvert and cool completely on racks. The cakes can be wrapped in plastic and stored at room temperature for up to 3 days.

FROSTINGS & FILLINGS

Use the chart on page 253 to determine the amounts needed to fill or frost four common tier sizes.

SWISS MERINGUE BUTTERCREAM
MAKES ABOUT 12 CUPS

With its silky smooth texture, buttery taste, and melt-in-your-mouth quality, this buttercream is a favorite frosting and filling. If making ahead of time, be sure to store it away from foods with strong odors.

3 cups sugar

12 large egg whites

2 pounds (8 sticks) unsalted butter, cut into tablespoons, at room temperature

2 teaspoons pure vanilla extract

1. Put the sugar and egg whites in the heat-proof bowl of an electric mixer, and set over a pan of simmering water. Whisk constantly until the sugar is dissolved and the mixture registers 140°F on an instant-read thermometer.

2. Transfer the bowl to an electric mixer fitted with the whisk attachment. Beat on medium-high speed until fluffy and cooled, about 10 minutes. Continue beating until stiff, glossy peaks form.

3. Reduce the speed to medium-low; add the butter by the tablespoon, beating well after each addition. Beat in the vanilla. The buttercream can be refrigerated in an airtight container for up to 1 week or frozen for up to 1 month. Bring to room temperature before using; beat on low speed until smooth, about 3 minutes.

COCONUT BUTTERCREAM
Follow the instructions for Swiss Meringue Buttercream, beating in 1 cup shredded unsweetened coconut with the vanilla in step 3.

WHITE CHOCOLATE BUTTERCREAM
MAKES ABOUT 9 CUPS

Make sure the white chocolate is cooled to room temperature before adding in step 3.

2½ cups sugar

10 large egg whites

2 pounds (8 sticks) unsalted butter, cut into tablespoons, at room temperature

2 teaspoons pure vanilla extract

1 pound best-quality white chocolate, melted and cooled

1. Put the sugar and egg whites in the heat-proof bowl of an electric mixer, and set over a pan of simmering water. Whisk constantly until the sugar is dissolved and the mixture registers 140°F on an instant-read thermometer.

2. Transfer the bowl to an electric mixer fitted with the whisk attachment; beat on medium-high until fluffy and cooled, about 10 minutes. Continue beating until stiff peaks form.

3. Reduce the speed to medium-low; add the butter by the tablespoon, beating well after each addition. Beat in the vanilla and white chocolate. Buttercream can be refrigerated in an airtight container for up to 1 week or frozen for up to 1 month. Bring to room temperature before using; beat on the lowest speed until smooth, about 3 minutes.

VANILLA CUSTARD BUTTERCREAM

MAKES ABOUT 13 CUPS

Because it is made with yolks as well as whites, this buttercream has a wonderfully silky texture and a richer, rounder flavor than Swiss Meringue Buttercream. Cakes that are frosted or filled with this buttercream should always be refrigerated for as long as possible until serving.

6 large eggs, separated

1½ cups sugar

2 cups whole milk

1 teaspoon pure vanilla extract

*6 cups (12 sticks) unsalted butter,
at room temperature*

1. Put the egg yolks and ½ cup of the sugar into the bowl of an electric mixer fitted with the whisk attachment; beat on high speed until pale and thickened, 2 to 3 minutes.

2. Bring the milk and vanilla to a boil in a medium saucepan. Remove from the heat. Whisk about one third of the liquid into the yolk mixture. Pour the mixture back into the pan with the remaining custard; whisk to combine. Cook over medium heat, stirring constantly, until the mixture registers 185°F on an instant-read thermometer. Remove from the heat; strain. Refrigerate until cool.

3. Put the butter into the bowl of an electric mixer fitted with the paddle attachment; mix on medium-high speed until pale and fluffy. Mix in the chilled custard.

4. Heat the egg whites and the remaining 1 cup sugar in the clean heat-proof bowl of an electric mixer set over a pan of simmering water, whisking constantly, until the sugar has dissolved. Attach the bowl to the mixer fitted with the whisk attachment; beat on high speed until stiff peaks form.

5. Add the egg-white mixture to the butter mixture; beat on medium-high speed until smooth. Refrigerate in an airtight container for up to 3 days; bring to room temperature, and beat before using.

COFFEE BUTTERCREAM

Follow the instructions for Vanilla Custard Buttercream, adding 5 tablespoons coffee extract at the end.

FRUIT-FLAVORED BUTTERCREAM

Follow the instructions for Vanilla Custard Buttercream, adding ½ cup strained puréed fruit (about 3 cups fruit: small berries can be left whole; slice larger fruit and peel if necessary) in step 5.

MINT BUTTERCREAM

Follow the instructions for Vanilla Custard Buttercream, adding 2 cups chopped mint leaves with the milk and vanilla in step 2. Tint the buttercream pale green.

CARAMEL BUTTERCREAM

Follow the instructions for Vanilla Custard Buttercream, adding 1½ cups Caramel–Cream Cheese Filling (page 243) in step 5.

SEVEN-MINUTE FROSTING
MAKES ABOUT 8 CUPS

When you want a pure white cake, this frosting is a good choice. It hardens quickly, so prepare it just before assembling the cake. The sugar syrup needs to be added to the egg whites as soon as the syrup reaches 230°F, so it's good to be beating the whites while heating the syrup.

1¾ cups sugar

2 tablespoons light corn syrup

6 large egg whites, at room temperature

1 teaspoon pure vanilla extract

1. Cook 1½ cups of the sugar, ¼ cup water, and the corn syrup in a small saucepan over medium heat, stirring occasionally, until the sugar is dissolved, about 4 minutes. Raise the heat to medium-high; cook, stirring, washing down the sides of the pan occasionally with a pastry brush dipped in water to prevent crystals from forming, until the mixture comes to a boil. Cook, without stirring, until the mixture registers 230°F on a candy thermometer, 4 to 8 minutes depending on the humidity. Remove from the heat.

2. Meanwhile, beat the egg whites on medium speed in the bowl of an electric mixer fitted with the whisk attachment until soft peaks form, 2 to 3 minutes. With the mixer running, add the remaining ¼ cup sugar in a slow, steady stream. Reduce the speed to medium-low, and carefully pour the hot syrup down the side of the bowl.

3. Beat on medium until the frosting is thick, shiny, and completely cooled, about 7 minutes. Mix in the vanilla. Use the frosting immediately.

WHITE CHOCOLATE FONDANT
MAKES ABOUT 2 POUNDS

The white chocolate gives fondant a softer texture, so you may need to use more cornstarch (or work in a cooler room) when rolling it out.

9 ounces best-quality white chocolate, finely chopped

1 ounce cocoa butter (see Sources, page 254)

7 tablespoons light corn syrup

1 pound rolled fondant (see Sources, page 254)

Cornstarch, for dusting, if needed

1. Bring a pan of water just to a boil; remove from the heat.

2. Put the chocolate and cocoa butter in a heat-proof bowl and set it over the pan; stir just until melted. Remove the bowl from the pan; stir in the corn syrup. Pour the mixture onto a sheet of plastic wrap; fold the sides in to cover completely. Let stand at room temperature overnight.

3. Knead the white chocolate mixture to soften, then knead it into rolled fondant until well incorporated (if it sticks, sprinkle the work surface with cornstarch). Wrap in plastic; let rest overnight. Before using, microwave the fondant on medium power for 5-second intervals until pliable.

CREAM CHEESE FROSTING
MAKES 9½ CUPS

4 packages (8 ounces each) cream cheese, at room temperature

1 teaspoon pure vanilla extract

*8 tablespoons (1 stick) unsalted butter,
softened and cut into pieces*

2 pounds confectioners' sugar, sifted

1. Mix cream cheese and vanilla on medium speed in the bowl of an electric mixer fitted with the paddle attachment until creamy and light, 2 minutes. With mixer running, gradually add butter; mix until combined.

2. Reduce speed to low; gradually mix in sugar until combined. If not using immediately, refrigerate, covered, up to 3 days; bring to room temperature and beat until smooth before using.

FUDGE FROSTING
MAKES ABOUT 3½ CUPS

Cocoa powder gives this frosting a deep chocolate flavor. This recipe can be doubled.

3½ cups confectioners' sugar

1 cup unsweetened cocoa powder

*12 tablespoons (1½ sticks) unsalted butter,
at room temperature*

½ cup milk, at room temperature

2 teaspoons pure vanilla extract

Sift the confectioners' sugar and cocoa powder into the bowl of an electric mixer fitted with the paddle attachment. Add the butter, milk, and vanilla; beat until smooth. If not using immediately, store the frosting in an airtight container in the refrigerator. Before using, bring the frosting to room temperature, and beat until smooth.

SHINY CHOCOLATE GLAZE
MAKES 8 CUPS

This glaze covers the Chocolate Kumquat Cake on page 176. You can make this recipe up to 3 days in advance. Refrigerate it in an airtight container with plastic wrap directly on the surface, and bring to room temperature before using.

1 quarter-ounce package unflavored powdered gelatin

½ cup cold water

3¾ cups sugar

3 12-ounce jars apricot preserves, puréed

1½ cups best-quality cocoa powder

¾ cup finely chopped semisweet chocolate

5 ounces unsweetened chocolate, chopped

1. Soften the gelatin by sprinkling it over the ½ cup cold water. Let stand for 5 minutes.

2. Using a medium pan over medium-high heat, bring 1½ cups water, the sugar, and the preserves to a boil. Add the gelatin mixture, cocoa, chocolate chips, and chocolate. Return to a boil; stir constantly for 2 minutes. Remove from the heat. Whisk until smooth, about 3 minutes; strain through a fine sieve.

PASTRY CREAM
MAKES 1 QUART

This pastry cream is a popular filling for wedding cakes. Try varying the flavor to complement your choice of cake and frosting by infusing the milk with ingredients such as orange, lime, or lemon zest, or cinnamon, star anise, or cardamom. Be sure to make a frosting dam on each cake layer before filling with pastry cream.

1 quart milk

1 cup sugar

2 vanilla beans, split lengthwise

½ cup cornstarch

4 large whole eggs

4 large egg yolks

8 tablespoons (1 stick) unsalted butter, cut into small pieces

1. In a medium saucepan, combine the milk and ½ cup of the sugar. Scrape in the vanilla seeds, and add the pods. Bring the mixture to a boil over medium-high heat, stirring occasionally. Remove from the heat, and cover. Set aside for 10 minutes; discard the vanilla pod.

2. Have an ice-water bath ready. In a small bowl, mix together the remaining ½ cup sugar with the cornstarch. In a medium bowl, whisk together the eggs and egg yolks; add the sugar mixture, and continue whisking until pale yellow.

3. Return the milk mixture to a boil. Slowly ladle half of the boiling milk mixture into the egg-yolk mixture, whisking constantly. Transfer this new mixture back to the saucepan.

4. Set the pan over medium heat, whisking constantly and scraping the sides and edges of the pan. Once the mixture comes to a boil, whisk vigorously until thick, about 1½ minutes.

5. Remove the pan from the heat. Strain the cream through a fine sieve into a medium bowl set over the ice-water bath; use a rubber spatula to extract as much liquid as possible. Whisk the butter, piece by piece, into the pastry cream while still warm. Let cool completely. Lay plastic wrap directly on the surface of the pastry cream to prevent a skin from forming; wrap the bowl tightly. Store the pastry cream in the refrigerator for up to 3 days.

WHITE CHOCOLATE MOUSSE
MAKES ABOUT 4 CUPS

A light and airy mousse is a delicious alternative to other types of fillings, and pairs especially well with fresh fruit. Be sure to create a frosting dam before filling layers with any mousse, and always keep filled cakes in the refrigerator.

1½ teaspoons unflavored powdered gelatin

¼ cup cold water

12 ounces best-quality white chocolate, coarsely chopped

2 cups cold heavy cream

1. Dissolve the gelatin in the cold water in a small bowl. Let stand for 5 minutes.

2. Pulse the white chocolate in a food processor until finely chopped. Bring ¾ cup of the cream just to a boil in a small saucepan over medium-high heat. Add the gelatin mixture; stir to dissolve, about 30 seconds.

3. With the machine running, add the cream mixture to the white chocolate; process until smooth. Transfer the mixture to a medium bowl, cover with plastic wrap; chill until thick enough to hold a ribbon on the surface when drizzled, about 30 minutes.

4. Beat the remaining 1¼ cups cream until almost stiff peaks form. Fold a third of the cream into the white chocolate mixture, then the rest. Chill until almost firm and set, 25 to 30 minutes. Whisk the mousse until smooth, and use immediately.

CARAMEL-CREAM CHEESE FILLING
MAKES ABOUT 4 CUPS

Caramel is a natural partner for apple or chocolate cakes, and is also delicious with most any butter cake.

4½ cups sugar

½ cup (1 stick) unsalted butter, at room temperature

1½ cups cream cheese, at room temperature, cut into small pieces

---

1. Put sugar and ⅔ cup water in a medium, heavy saucepan. Cook over medium-high heat, stirring occasionally, until sugar has dissolved. Continue to cook, without stirring, until syrup comes to a boil, washing down sides of pan with a wet pastry brush to prevent crystals from forming. Let boil, swirling pan occasionally, until mixture turns medium amber. Remove from heat.

2. Whisk in butter and cream cheese. Let mixture cool, stirring occasionally. Transfer to an airtight container. Refrigerate overnight; beat until thick enough to hold a ribbon on the surface before using.

MASCARPONE CREAM FILLING
MAKES ABOUT 4 CUPS

This recipe can be doubled. The filling can be refrigerated, covered, for up to 3 days; whisk until stiff before using.

2 cups mascarpone cheese, at room temperature

2 tablespoons sugar

¾ cup heavy cream

In the bowl of an electric mixer fitted with the whisk attachment, beat the mascarpone and sugar on medium speed until combined. Add the cream; beat until stiff peaks form.

MARZIPAN
MAKES ABOUT 2½ POUNDS

Marzipan is best used the day it is made. Keep covered with plastic wrap to prevent it from drying out. You can also buy packaged marzipan instead of making your own.

1 pound almond paste

1 pound confectioners' sugar

⅓ cup light corn syrup

In a food processor, pulse the almond paste and confectioners' sugar until combined. Add the corn syrup; pulse 8 times more, or until the mixture holds together when pressed. Transfer to a clean work surface; knead until the mixture forms a smooth dough. Wrap tightly in plastic wrap.

ROYAL ICING
MAKES ABOUT 2½ CUPS

This versatile icing is an essential part of any decorator's repertoire. When thick and dense, it is good for piping; thinned with water, it is used for flooding. Always give it a good stir before putting the icing in a pastry bag.

5 tablespoons meringue powder

1 pound confectioners' sugar

Put the meringue powder and sugar into the bowl of an electric mixer fitted with the paddle attachment; mix on low speed until combined, gradually adding a scant ½ cup water. Increase speed to high and beat for about 7 minutes. Add additional sugar or water to reach the desired consistency. Use immediately.

EMBELLISHMENTS & EXTRAS

These recipes are for some of the accents that make a cake particularly distinctive.

CARAMEL SAUCE

MAKES 1 CUP

You will need 19 batches of caramel sauce to serve 150 guests. This recipe can easily be multiplied.

1 cup sugar

¼ teaspoon salt

½ cup heavy cream

2 tablespoons butter

½ teaspoon pure vanilla extract

---

1. Stir together sugar, salt, and ¼ cup water in a small saucepan. Cook over medium heat, washing down sides of pan with a wet pastry brush to prevent crystals from forming, until mixture turns medium amber.

2. Remove from heat; carefully stir in cream (caramel will steam). Add butter; stir until combined. Let cool to room temperature; stir in vanilla. If not using immediately, refrigerate in an airtight container up to 2 weeks. Reheat, and let cool to room temperature before serving.

CHOCOLATE PETALS

MAKES ABOUT 110 PETALS

To make the petals on the cake on page 137, you will need a cake ring measuring 2¾ inches wide by 2 inches high. The size of the petals will depend on the temperature of the chocolate and the angle of the mold as it scrapes across the chocolate.

The petals can be stored for up to 1 week in a tightly sealed container; keep them in a single layer on parchment paper, and store in an air-conditioned room away from direct heat or sunlight. Do not refrigerate.

3 blocks (each 2 pounds, 3 ounces)
best-quality milk chocolate, such as Valrhona

---

1. Work with one block at a time. Place the block inside a shallow baking pan; line a second pan with parchment paper. Use a heat lamp (or a gooseneck lamp) to slightly warm the chocolate, being careful not to melt it. (Adjust the distance between the lamp and chocolate as necessary.)

2. Steady the pan in place with one hand. Using the ring mold, scrape the block from top to bottom, pressing lightly, forming curls. Carefully transfer the petals to a parchment-lined baking sheet; if your hands are too warm to handle the petals without melting them, use a wooden skewer.

GINGER-INFUSED SIMPLE SYRUP
MAKES 1¾ CUPS

This recipe can be made two weeks in advance.
Refrigerate in an airtight container.

1½ cups sugar

*1 2-by-2-inch piece fresh ginger (about 2 ounces),
peeled and thinly sliced*

In a heavy-bottomed saucepan over high heat, stir the sugar, ginger, and 1½ cups water together until the sugar is dissolved. Bring to a boil. Reduce the heat to medium; simmer for 10 minutes. Remove from the heat, let cool completely, and strain.

MODELING CHOCOLATE
MAKES ABOUT 1 POUND

2 ounces cocoa butter

10½ ounces best-quality bittersweet chocolate, finely chopped

½ cup light corn syrup

Unsweetened cocoa powder, for dusting

1. Melt the cocoa butter in a small saucepan over low heat; let cool. Heat the chocolate in a heat-proof bowl set over a pan of simmering water until it registers 110°F to 115°F on a candy thermometer.

2. Heat the corn syrup in a small, heavy-bottomed saucepan over low heat until it registers 95°F on a candy thermometer; pour into the melted chocolate. Stir in the cooled cocoa butter. Set aside in a cool, dry place, stirring occasionally, until firm and pliable, 1½ to 2 hours.

3. Pat into a disk, and wrap tightly in plastic wrap. Refrigerate until firm, about 1 hour (or let stand at room temperature overnight). Transfer the modeling chocolate to a clean work surface lightly dusted with cocoa; knead until smooth. Use immediately, or wrap well in plastic wrap and store at room temperature for up to 1 month.

MERINGUE DISKS
MAKES 2 EACH 12-INCH, 10-INCH, 8-INCH, AND 6-INCH CIRCLES

You will need to bake the meringue in batches, preferably on a cool, dry day. The disks can be stacked and filled along with the cake layers for a bit of contrasting texture.

Vegetable oil cooking spray

8 recipes Simple Meringue (recipe follows)

1. Preheat the oven to 150°F. Draw two 12-inch circles, two 10-inch circles, two 8-inch circles, and two 6-inch circles on parchment paper. Turn the parchment over so the drawings do not mark the meringue disks during baking. Spray baking sheets with cooking spray and place parchment on top.

2. Spread the meringue inside the circles on the prepared parchment-lined baking sheets. The disks should be about 1 inch thick. Bake until crisp but not brown, 4 to 6 hours. Turn off the oven, and allow the meringues to remain in the oven at least 8 hours or overnight. The inside should remain chewy. Store cooled meringue disks in an airtight container or in a cool, dry place until ready to use. The disks can be baked up to 1 day in advance if the weather is cool and dry.

Approximate amounts for each tier size: 6-inch round: 2½ cups; 8-inch: 4 cups; 10-inch: 5½ cups; 12-inch: 8 cups

SIMPLE MERINGUE
MAKES 8 CUPS

8 large egg whites, at room temperature

½ teaspoon cream of tartar

2 cups superfine sugar

1. In the bowl of an electric mixer fitted with the whisk attachment, beat egg whites on low speed until foamy. Add cream of tartar, increase to medium speed, and beat until soft peaks form. Increase speed to high; add sugar 1 tablespoon at a time.

2. Beat until the peaks are stiff and glossy, about 6 minutes. Use meringue immediately. If it is overbeaten or not used immediately, air bubbles will weaken its structure when baked.

MERINGUE MUSHROOMS

For more realistic hues, we tinted some of the meringue with varying amounts of cocoa. See page 233 for the how-to.

Vegetable oil cooking spray

Swiss Meringue (recipe follows)

*3 tablespoons unsweetened cocoa powder, sifted,
plus more for dusting*

2 ounces bittersweet chocolate, finely chopped

3 ounces white chocolate, finely chopped

1. Preheat the oven to 200°F. Spray two or three rimmed baking sheets with cooking spray and line with parchment paper; set aside. Divide the meringue among three small bowls; set one aside. Fold 1 tablespoon of the cocoa into the second portion, and fold the remaining 2 tablespoons cocoa into the third portion. Place each portion in an 18-inch pastry bag fitted with a large round ½-inch tip. Pipe domes, ½ inch to 2 inches in diameter, onto the lined baking sheets, and flatten the tips with a damp fingertip. Pipe stems onto the baking sheets, pulling up to form a point. Make one stem to go with each "cap."

2. Bake in the upper and lower thirds of the oven, switching the positions of the sheets halfway through, for 1 hour; reduce the oven temperature to 175°F. Continue baking until the meringues are completely dry to the touch (they should peel off the sheet easily) but not browned, 45 to 60 minutes.

3. Melt the bittersweet chocolate, stirring occasionally, in a small heat-proof bowl over a pan of simmering water. Using a small offset spatula, spread the bottoms of the caps with a thin layer of dark chocolate, and let set. Melt the white chocolate in another heat-proof bowl set over a pan of simmering water. Let cool until thickened, and spread over the dark chocolate. Use a toothpick to draw lines from the center to the edge of the caps (to form the gills), and let set.

4. Using a paring knife, make a small hole in center of the underside of each coated cap. Dip the pointed end of each stem in the remaining white chocolate, and insert into a cap; let set. Store in airtight containers in a cool, dry place for up to 1 week. Just before decorating the cake, dust some of the mushroom caps with more cocoa powder.

SWISS MERINGUE

4 large egg whites

1 cup sugar

Pinch of cream of tartar

½ teaspoon pure vanilla extract

1. Fill a medium saucepan one-quarter full with water, and bring to a simmer over medium heat. Combine the egg whites, sugar, and cream of tartar in a heat-proof bowl of an electric mixer and place over the saucepan. Whisk constantly until the mixture registers 140°F on an instant-read thermometer and the sugar is dissolved, about 3 minutes.

2. Transfer the bowl to the mixer fitted with the whisk attachment; starting on low speed and gradually increasing to high, whisk the mixture until the meringue is cool, and stiff, glossy peaks form, about 10 minutes. Mix in the vanilla.

LEMON MADELEINES

These traditional French cakes are best the day they are made, but they can be refrigerated in a single layer in an airtight container for up to three days; bring to room temperature before serving.

*¾ cup (1½ sticks) unsalted butter, melted,
plus more for the pan*

1½ cups sifted cake flour (not self-rising)

½ teaspoon baking powder

¼ teaspoon salt

3 large whole eggs

2 large egg yolks

¾ cup granulated sugar

1 teaspoon pure vanilla extract

2 tablespoons finely grated lemon zest

2 tablespoons freshly squeezed lemon juice

1. Preheat the oven to 400°F. Lightly butter a madeleine pan, and set aside. Into a medium bowl, sift together the flour, baking powder, and salt. Set aside.

2. In the bowl of an electric mixer fitted with the whisk attachment, beat the whole eggs, egg yolks, granulated sugar, vanilla, and lemon zest and juice until thick and pale, about 5 minutes. Beat in the melted butter. Using a rubber spatula, gently fold the flour mixture into the egg mixture; let rest for 30 minutes at room temperature.

3. Pour the batter into the prepared pan, filling the molds three-quarters full. Bake until the cakes are crisp and golden around the edges, 7 to 8 minutes. Transfer the pan to a wire rack to cool slightly before unmolding the cakes onto the rack (invert them so they are flat-side down) to cool completely.

CROQUEMBOUCHE

SERVES 14

This recipe is for the cake shown on page 164; you can follow the same steps to create a larger version using more puffs. Freeze the extra puffs for another time; be sure to wrap them well to prevent them from absorbing odors. Fill them with any custard or creamy filling.

½ cup milk

8 tablespoons (1 stick) unsalted butter

1 teaspoon coarse salt

1 cup sifted all-purpose flour

5 large whole eggs

1 large egg yolk

¼ cup heavy cream

Passion-Fruit Mousse (recipe follows)

Nougat (recipe follows)

Oil, for parchment paper

Caramel (recipe follows)

Tuile Banners (recipe follows)

Spun Sugar (recipe follows)

1. Preheat the oven to 400°F. Line three baking sheets with parchment paper; set aside.

2. In a medium saucepan, combine the milk, butter, salt, and ½ cup water. Bring to a boil over medium-high heat; stir in the flour. Stir constantly until the mixture pulls away from the sides of the pan and becomes stiff, about 5 minutes. Remove from the heat; transfer to the bowl of an electric mixer. Using the paddle attachment, mix on low speed for about 1 minute. With the mixer running, add the whole eggs, one at a time, beating well between additions. Transfer the dough to a pastry bag fitted with a ¼-inch plain round tip (Ateco #802).

3. In a small bowl, combine the egg yolk with the heavy cream for an egg wash. Pipe uniform amounts of dough onto the prepared baking sheets, spacing them 1 inch apart (about 50 puffs on each sheet). Gently brush the tops with the egg wash. Bake until the puffs are golden brown, about 15 minutes. Transfer to a wire rack to cool.

4. Using a toothpick or skewer, poke a small hole in the bottom of each puff. Fill the puffs with the passion-fruit mousse. Place the filled puffs onto a baking sheet; place in the refrigerator until ready to use.

5. Prepare the nougat base and triangles; set aside. Trace the bottom of a 5-inch tart pan on a piece of lightly oiled parchment; set aside. Prepare the caramel; using hot caramel, attach the nougat triangles at a 25-degree angle to the base's edge, forming a crown.

6. Working quickly, partially dip the filled puffs one at a time in the caramel, then adhere one puff to the next. Using the puffs, build an 8-inch-tall cone-shaped tower; its base should be inside the parchment circle (build it on the parchment so the hot caramel does not melt the crown). You will use about 80 puffs (any remaining puffs can be used for serving). Transfer the completed tower to the nougat crown. Decorate with a tuile banner and spun sugar.

PASSION-FRUIT MOUSSE
MAKES 3 CUPS

3 large eggs

⅓ cup sugar

⅓ cup passion-fruit purée

1 tablespoon unsalted butter

¼ cup fresh orange juice

2 teaspoons powdered gelatin

1 cup heavy cream

1. Fill a medium bowl with ice water; set aside. In a small nonreactive saucepan, combine the eggs, sugar, and passion-fruit purée. Cook, stirring constantly, over medium-low heat until the mixture thickens enough to coat the back of a spoon, about 3 minutes. Remove from the heat, immediately add the butter, and stir well to combine.

2. In a medium saucepan, combine the orange juice and 2 tablespoons cold water. Sprinkle the gelatin over the orange-juice mixture; let stand for 5 minutes. Place over low heat until the gelatin is completely dissolved, about 2 minutes.

3. Pour the passion-fruit mixture through a fine sieve or chinois into a nonreactive bowl. Stir in the gelatin mixture. Place the bowl over the ice water; whisk constantly until the mixture has cooled.

4. In a chilled bowl, whip the heavy cream until stiff peaks form, about 3 minutes. Whisk one third of the whipped cream into the passion-fruit mixture. Then, in two additions, fold the lightened passion-fruit mixture into the remaining whipped cream. Transfer the mixture to a pastry bag fitted with a round (Ateco #3) tip; set aside.

NOUGAT
MAKES ENOUGH FOR I CROWN

1 cup sugar

Juice of ½ lemon (2 tablespoons)

1½ cups finely chopped toasted almonds

Vegetable oil

1. Preheat the oven to 300°F. In a medium saucepan, combine the sugar and the lemon juice. Place over medium heat; bring to a boil, without stirring. Clip on a candy thermometer, and continue to boil until the mixture reaches 340°F. Remove from the heat, and immediately stir in the almonds.

2. Pour the mixture onto an oiled Silpat (or other nonstick baking mat) or countertop, and spread out with an oiled offset spatula. Fold the nougat over itself several times to cool slightly. While it is still warm, roll it out into a 10-inch disk with an oiled rolling pin.

3. Lightly oil a 6-inch fluted tart pan; place on an oiled baking sheet. Cut an 8-inch round from the nougat disk, and transfer the round to the tart pan, pressing it into the pan. Transfer the tart pan to the oven until the nougat becomes pliable, about 2 minutes. Press the edge of the nougat into the flutes of the tart pan, then trim any excess. Set aside.

4. Using a ruler and knife, cut the remaining nougat into 15 one-inch equilateral triangles. If the nougat becomes too stiff, place it back on a baking sheet and return it to the oven for a few minutes to soften. Set the triangles aside to cool completely.

CARAMEL
MAKES I½ CUPS

2 cups sugar

2 tablespoons light corn syrup

Fill a large bowl (or the sink) with ice water. In a small saucepan, heat the sugar, corn syrup, and ⅔ cup water without stirring, until the mixture comes to a boil. Clip on a candy thermometer; continue to boil until the mixture reaches 340°F. Remove from the heat; dip the pan into the ice bath to stop the caramel from cooking. Use immediately. If the caramel begins to harden, return it to the heat until it is thick but pourable.

CROQUEMBOUCHE HOW-TOS

{1} MAKING NOUGAT A nougatine crown, a mixture of chopped nuts and caramel, is the traditional base for a croquembouche. Nougat remains malleable for a while as it cools, allowing it to be manipulated into shapes. Here, it is formed in a tart shell. When cool, it is unmolded and turned upside down to form the base. Triangles of nougat are cut from another piece and attached to the base with still-warm caramel. The nougatine crown is best made on a clear, dry day; humidity makes the nougat sticky and difficult to work with.

{2} MAKING TUILE BANNERS To make these delicate French wafers, spread a thin layer of batter onto a baking sheet through a stencil cut from a piece of craft foam. Pipe chocolate batter onto the wet tuile. When baked, the edges turn golden brown. The cookies can be draped while warm over rolling pins to form undulating shapes. Be sure to make extra banners, as they are quite fragile and break easily.

{3} MAKING A SPUN-SUGAR CROWN Spun sugar is made from sugar, corn syrup, and a bit of beeswax to keep the sugar flexible. To make the necessary tool, which will allow the maximum number of strands to be spun, snip looped ends of a wire whisk with wire cutters. Then "throw" the heated sugar from the whisk onto a wooden laundry rack, forming long, thin strands. (Wooden spoons hanging over the edge of a counter also work.) Spun sugar may look brittle, but its strands can be wrapped around the croquembouche.

TUILE BANNERS
MAKES 16

Make extra banners; they are quite fragile.

1 piece of foam board (12 by 18 inches)

Nonstick cooking spray

7½ tablespoons unsalted butter

6 large egg whites

1½ cups superfine sugar

1¼ cups all-purpose flour, sifted

Pinch of salt

5 tablespoons heavy cream

1 teaspoon pure almond extract

¼ cup Dutch-process cocoa powder

FOR THE ALMOND BATTER

1. Draw a banner onto the foam board; cut out a stencil with a utility knife. Set the stencil aside.

2. Preheat the oven to 400°F. Line a baking sheet with a Silpat or other nonstick baking mat. Coat with cooking spray. Melt 5 tablespoons of the butter in a saucepan over low heat; set aside.

3. In the bowl of an electric mixer fitted with the paddle attachment, combine four of the egg whites and 1 cup sugar; beat on medium for 30 seconds. Add 1 cup flour and the salt; mix well. Add the melted butter, 3 tablespoons cream, and the almond extract; beat until combined, 1 minute.

4. Transfer the batter to an airtight container; refrigerate until chilled, about 15 minutes.

FOR THE CHOCOLATE BATTER

1. In a saucepan over low heat, melt the remaining 2½ tablespoons butter; set aside.

2. In the bowl of an electric mixer fitted with the paddle attachment, combine the remaining 2 egg whites and ½ cup sugar. Beat on medium until combined, about 30 seconds. Add the remaining ¼ cup flour and the cocoa powder; beat well. Pour in the melted butter and the remaining 2 tablespoons heavy cream. Beat on medium until combined, about 1 minute. Transfer to a pastry bag fitted with a fine-holed round (Ateco #1) tip; set aside.

3. Lay two rolling pins parallel to one another on a work surface. Place the foam-board stencil on the Silpat. Using an offset spatula, spread the chilled almond batter inside the stencil on the Silpat. Lift the stencil, and repeat several more times on the Silpat, wiping the stencil after each use. With the chocolate batter, pipe out desired words directly onto the banners.

4. Bake four banners at a time, until the edges begin to brown, about 6 minutes. Carefully remove from the baking sheet; drape over two rolling pins. Remove when cooled, about 2 minutes. Repeat until all the batter is used. Store banners in a single layer in an airtight container until ready to use.

SPUN SUGAR
MAKES ENOUGH FOR 1 CROQUEMBOUCHE

The spun sugar is best made in a cool, dry
work area up to 1 hour before serving. The beeswax
keeps the spun-sugar strands pliable.

Vegetable oil

½ cup sugar

⅓ cup light corn syrup

1 teaspoon grated beeswax (see Sources, page 254)

1. Lightly oil a wooden laundry rack (or two wooden spoons securely taped to your work surface). Cover the floor with newspaper or parchment paper.

2. In a small saucepan, combine the sugar and the corn syrup. Bring the mixture to a boil, and clip on a candy thermometer. Boil the mixture until it turns a pale amber color; the thermometer should read 265°F. Remove from the heat, and let cool for 2 minutes. Stir in the beeswax.

3. Cool the mixture, stirring occasionally, until 150°F. Stand on a step stool so you are about 2 feet above your work surface. Using a cut whisk or two forks, side by side, dip into the warm mixture and wave the sugar back and forth over a clean wooden drying rack, allowing the strands to fall in long, thin threads. Wrap the strands around the croquembouche as soon as possible.

devotion

devotion

promise

love

cherish

trust

I do

respect

BAKERS' GUIDELINES

This chart is designed to help you in two ways: First, you can use it as a guide for baking the cakes in this section; you can also use it to adapt many of the recipes in the Album of Cakes, which have specific instructions for making the assembled cake as shown. (For example, the Chocolate Butter Cake on page 114 was baked in hexagonal cake pans to make the Pink Cherry Blossom Cake; so you can follow the guidelines here for making a different size and shape cake.) We chose four common tier sizes (6-, 8-, 10-, and 12-inch); except for the dacquoise, the cakes were baked in 3-inch-deep (professional) round cake pans, and the batter amounts are enough to fill the pan two-thirds full. The amounts given are estimates and should only be used as a guide. Always rely on visual cues (such as inserting a cake tester in the middle) to determine when the cakes are ready; it is also a good idea to check any cake after an hour, regardless of our suggested times, as ovens can vary widely. An oven thermometer will help ensure accuracy.

CAKES	6-INCH	8-INCH	10-INCH	12-INCH
ALMOND-CORNMEAL POUND CAKE	4 cups; 1 hour	7 cups; 1 hour 10 minutes	10 cups; 1 hour 15 minutes	15 cups; 1 hour 25 minutes
ALMOND DACQUOISE	1 cup; 1 hour 35 minutes	2 cups; 1 hour 45 minutes	3 cups; 2 hours	4 cups; 2 hours
APPLE CAKE	3½ cups; 1 hour	6½ cups; 1 hour 15 minutes	9 cups; 1 hour 15 minutes	14 cups; 1 hour 45 minutes
BUTTER CAKES	3 cups; 30 minutes	5 cups; 40 minutes	8 cups; 1 hour 5 minutes	11 cups; 1 hour 15 minutes
CARROT CAKE	3 cups; 1 hour 20 minutes	5 cups; 1 hour 25 minutes	7 cups; 1 hour 35 minutes	10 cups; 1 hour 40 minutes
COCONUT CAKE	4 cups; 55 minutes	7 cups; 1 hour	11 cups; 1 hour 5 minutes	15 cups; 1 hour 10 minutes
DEVIL'S FOOD CAKE	3½ cups; 1 hour	6½ cups; 1 hour 15 minutes	9½ cups; 1 hour 20 minutes	14 cups; 1 hour 25 minutes
LEMON POPPY SEED POUND CAKE	6 cups; 1 hour	9 cups; 1 hour 30 minutes	12 cups; 1 hour 30 minutes	15 cups; 2 hours
MARBLE CAKE	4 cups; 50 minutes	6½ cups; 55 minutes	9 cups; 1 hour	14½ cups; 1 hour 10 minutes
MOCHA SPICE CAKE	3½ cups; 1 hour 15 minutes	6 cups; 1 hour	10 cups; 1 hour 50 minutes	12 cups; 1 hour 10 minutes
RED VELVET CAKE	3¼ cups; 55 minutes	5½ cups; 1 hour 5 minutes	9 cups; 1 hour 20 minutes	12¼ cups; 1 hour 25 minutes
VANILLA-BEAN SPONGE CAKES	3½ cups; 40 minutes	5½ cups; 45 minutes	8½ cups; 50 minutes	11 cups; 1 hour 10 minutes
YELLOW CAKE	3½ cups; 1 hour	6½ cups; 1 hour 10 minutes	9½ cups; 1 hour 5 minutes	15 cups; 1 hour 35 minutes

The amounts provided are for a standard two-layer 4-inch-tall tier, filled with a ¼-inch thick layer.

FROSTINGS & FILLINGS

	6-INCH	8-INCH	10-INCH	12-INCH
BUTTERCREAMS	¾ cup to fill; 1½ cups to frost	1¼ cups to fill; 2 cups to frost	2½ cups to fill; 3½ cups to frost	3 cups to fill; 4¼ cups to frost
CARAMEL–CREAM CHEESE FILLING	½ cup to fill	1 cup to fill	2½ cups to fill	3¼ cups to fill
CREAM CHEESE FROSTING	½ cup to fill; 1½ cups to frost	1 cup to fill; 2½ cups to frost	2½ cups to fill; 3½ cups to frost	3¼ cups to fill; 4¾ cups to frost
FUDGE FROSTING	½ cup to fill; 1¾ cups to frost	1 cup to fill; 2½ cups to frost	1½ cups to fill; 3 cups to frost	2½ cups to fill; 4¾ cups to frost
ITALIAN MERINGUE	¾ cup to fill; 1½ cups to frost	1¼ cups to fill; 2 cups to frost	2½ cups to fill; 3½ cups to frost	3 cups to fill; 4¼ cups to frost
LEMON CURD	½ cup to fill	1 cup to fill	1½ cups to fill	2 cups to fill
MARZIPAN	1½ pounds to cover	2 pounds to cover	2½ pounds to cover	3 pounds to cover
MASCARPONE CREAM FILLING	¾ cup to fill	1¼ cups to fill	2¼ cups to fill	3¼ cups to fill
PASTRY CREAM	½ cup to fill	1 cup to fill	1½ cups to fill	2 cups to fill
SEVEN-MINUTE FROSTING	¾ cup to fill; 1½ cups to frost	1¼ cups to fill; 2 cups to frost	2½ cups to fill; 3½ cups to frost	3 cups to fill; 4¼ cups to frost
SHINY CHOCOLATE GLAZE	1 cup to frost	1½ cups to frost	2 cups to frost	3 cups to frost
WHIPPED CHOCOLATE GANACHE	1 cup to fill	1¾ cups to fill	2½ cups to fill	3½ cups to fill
WHITE CHOCOLATE FONDANT	1½ pounds to cover	2 pounds to cover	2½ pounds to cover	3 pounds to cover
WHITE CHOCOLATE MOUSSE	½ cup to fill	1 cup to fill	2 cups to fill	3 cups to fill

SOURCES

BAKING AND DECORATING SUPPLIES

A. L. BAZZINI
200 Food Center Drive
Bronx, NY 10474
212-334-1280, 800-228-0172
www.bazzininuts.com
Almond paste and nuts.

BERYL'S
P.O. Box 1584
North Springfield, VA 22151
703-256-6951, 800-488-2749
www.beryls.com
Almond paste; cake boxes; cocoa butter; bench scrapers; gum paste; marzipan; meringue powder; nonstick boards; pastry bags, tips, and couplers; pastillage; petal dust; ribbons; rolled fondant; scallop cutter; small rolling pins.

BRIDGE KITCHENWARE
711 Third Avenue
New York, NY 10017
800-274-3445, 212-688-4220
www.bridgekitchenware.com
Wide supply of general and specialty baking supplies.

BROADWAY PANHANDLER
65 E. Eighth Street
New York, NY 10003
212-966-3434
www.broadwaypanhandler.com
Wide supply of general and specialty baking supplies.

CHOCOLATESOURCE.COM
9 Crest Road
Wellesley, MA 02482
800-214-4926
www.chocolatesource.com
High-quality chocolate, including Callebaut, Valrhona, and Scharffen Berger.

HYMAN HENDLER AND SONS
67 W. 38th Street
New York, NY 10018
212-704-4237
Ribbon.

J.B. PRINCE, NY
36 E. 31st Street
New York, NY 10016
800-473-0577
www.jbprince.com
Acetate roll; leaf cutters; pastry wheels; rotating cake table; wood-grain rocker tool.

KALUSTYAN'S
123 Lexington Avenue
New York, NY 10016
800-352-3451, 212-685-3451
www.kalustyans.com
Shredded unsweetened coconut; unsweetened coconut chips.

MANIFESTO LETTERPRESS
116 Pleasant Street, Eastworks-201/203
Easthampton, MA 01027
877-529-0009
www.manifestopress.com
Paper goods and custom letterpress services.

MASTERSTROKE CANADA
866-249-7677
www.masterstrokecanada.com
Ribbon.

MEADOWSWEETS
173 Kramer Road
Middleburgh, NY 12122
888-827-6477
www.candiedflowers.com
Crystallized flowers.

MICHAEL'S
Call or check website for store locations.
800-642-4235
www.michaels.com
Florist foam, wire, and tape, and general craft supplies.

M & J TRIMMING
1008 Sixth Avenue
New York, NY 10018
800-965-8746
www.mjtrim.com
Ribbon.

MOKUBA, NY
55 W. 39th Street
New York, NY 10018
212-869-8900
www.mokubany.com
Ribbon.

NEW YORK CAKE AND BAKING SUPPLIES
56 W. 22nd Street
New York, NY 10010
800-942-2539, 212-675-2253
www.nycake.com
Wide supply of general and specialty baking supplies.

PASTRY CHEF CENTRAL
1355 West Palmetto Park Road
Suite 302
Boca Raton, FL 33486
888-750-2433, 561-999-9483
www.pastrychef.com
Wide supply of general and specialty baking supplies.

PEARL PAINT
Call or check website for store locations.
212-431-7932, 800-451-7327
www.pearlpaint.com
³⁄₁₆-inch-thick foam board.

PFEIL AND HOLING
58-15 Northern Blvd.
Woodside, NY 11377
800-247-7955, 718-545-4500
www.cakedec.com
Wide supply of general and specialty baking supplies.

DENISE SHARP
of Studio D. Sharp
www.studiodsharp.com
Paper ornaments and cake toppers.

SOS CHEFS
104 Avenue B
New York, NY 10009
212-505-5813
www.sos-chefs.com
Cherries in kirsch brandy; beeswax.

STAMPWORX 2000
36 East 29th Street
2nd floor
New York, NY
800-998-7826
www.stampworx2000.biz
Custom-made rubber stamps.

SUGARCRAFT
2715 Dixie Highway
Hamilton, OH 45015
513-896-7089
www.sugarcraft.com
Coating chocolate; chocolate molds; coloring dusts (including luster, pearl, petal, and sparkle dusts); fondant cutters and embossers; gel-paste food colors; gum-paste flowers; floral tape and wire; royal-icing flowers.

VOSGES HAUT-CHOCOLAT
888-301-9866
www.vosgeschocotate.com
Gourmet chocolate, truffles, cakes, and wedding favors.

WENDY KROMER SPECIALTY CONFECTIONS
137 E. Water Street
Sandusky, OH 44870
419-609-0450
www.wendykromer.com.
Gum-paste flowers and songbirds; fondant bows; marzipan cherries; marzipan forest cake kit.

RON BEN-ISRAEL
Ron Ben-Israel Cakes,
New York
212-625-3369
www.weddingcakes.com

SAMANTHA CONNELL
917-312-9972

SAM GODFREY
Perfect Endings,
Napa, CA
707-259-0500
www.perfectendings.com

CHERYL KLEINMAN
Cheryl Kleinman Cakes,
Brooklyn, NY
718-237-2271

WENDY KROMER
Wendy Kromer Specialty Confections,
Sandusky, OH
419-609-0450
www.wendykromer.com.

ELIZABETH LOUDEN
856-428-3615

SANDEE MARTENSEN
914-273-4397

OHEKA CASTLE,
Huntington, NY
631-659-1400
www.oheka.com

ONE & ONLY OCEAN CLUB
Dune Restaurant, Bahamas
www.oneandonlyresorts.com

LOURDES PADILLA
Lourdes Padilla Wedding Cakes,
Guaynabo, Puerto Rico
787-798-1934
www.lourdespadillaweddingcakes.com

CLAIRE PEREZ
561-801-0297

APRIL REED
April Reed Cake Designs of New York
212-358-7071
www.aprilreed.com

LIZ STONE
Cornerstone Caterers,
Rye, NY
914-967-0035
www.cornerstonecaterers.com

GAIL WATSON
Gail Watson Custom Cakes,
New York
877-867-5088
www.gailwatsoncake.com

SYLVIA WEINSTOCK
Sylvia Weinstock Cakes & Ltd.
New York
212-925-6698
www.sylviaweinstock.com

ACKNOWLEDGMENTS

IT TAKES MUCH MORE THAN FLOUR, BUTTER, EGGS, and sugar to make a wedding cake. In fact, almost every cake that graces the pages of *Martha Stewart Weddings* represents the collaboration of many creative people, and I would like to thank those whose efforts have gone into making these cakes (and this book) as beautiful as they are.

Wendy Kromer is a true artist with a pastry bag, and this volume would not exist without her, so, Wendy, thank you for all the contributions you have made to *Martha Stewart Weddings* since 1995. Thank you also to editorial director Darcy Miller, who has run our *Weddings* business with grace and style since almost the beginning. For overseeing the editorial creation of this book, sincere thanks to special projects editor in chief Amy Conway. Brooke Hellewell Reynolds created a design as luscious and elegant as the cakes themselves. Creative director Eric A. Pike and art director William van Roden provided valuable guidance at every stage. Evelyn Battaglia's expertise as both an editor and a baker was indispensable; she helped shape the book from the start and brought clarity to each page.

For every issue of *Martha Stewart Weddings,* our art directors, stylists, and food editors are deeply involved in the creation of the cakes. They come up with clever concepts, design many of the desserts, create imaginative settings, and mix up batch after batch of batter and buttercream. Right down to the last dot of icing and the ribbon on the cake stand, their creativity and fine attention to detail are evident in each photograph. When it comes to help with baking and decorating the cakes, we turn to editorial director of food and entertaining, Lucinda Scala Quinn, and her team, including food editor Jennifer Aaronson, an excellent baker herself, and talented colleagues Shira Bocar, Brittany Williams, and Avery Wittkamp. For their amazingly creative ideas for many of the cakes and the settings in the book (and all the hard work that goes into executing them), very special thanks to Alexa Mulvihill, Jayme Smith, Susan

Spungen, Rebecca Thuss, and Theresa Canning Zast (who also helped to create some beautiful pictures just for this book).

Many thanks also to other contributors, past and present: John Barricelli, Lynn Butler Beling, Randi Brookman-Harris, Ellen Burnie, Livia Cetti, Kate Francis, Linda Lee, Sara Neumeier, Genevieve Panuska, Claire Perez, Hayat Pineiro, Bergren Rameson, Wendy Sidewater, Sharon Slaughter, and Robin Valarik. And thanks, too, to Hilary Sterne, editor in chief of *Martha Stewart Weddings.*

We are fortunate to work with many master bakers, among them Ron Ben-Israel, Gail Watson, and Sylvia Weinstock. They each have several creations in this book, and we are thrilled to share their vision and expertise with brides all over the country.

Ellen Morrissey provided advice throughout the process of creating this book. Amber Blakesley directed additional photo shoots beautifully. Kimberly Fusaro brought her way with words to the project, and Robb Riedel was instrumental in keeping everyone on track throughout. Denise Clappi, as always, solved problems along the way. Emily Burns, Andrea Cowsert, Yasemin Emory, Lori Key, and Jennifer Miranda took care of countless details. And Fritz Karch and Quy Nguyen kindly helped us track down some great cake toppers.

Heartfelt thanks, also, to the photographers whose work appears here (see their names opposite), and to our photo department, including Heloise Goodman, Andrea Bakacs, Mary Cahill, Alison Vanek Devine, and Joni Noe. We also appreciate the hard work of our EVP of print production, Dora Braschi Cardinale, and her colleagues George D. Planding and Lisa Fuchs.

As always, our executive team of Gael Towey, Margaret Roach, and Lauren Podlach Stanich lent valuable support to the project. And a very sincere thank-you, too, to our longtime friends and colleagues at Clarkson Potter: Jenny Frost, Lauren Shakely, Doris Cooper, Rica Allannic, Jane Treuhaft, Amy Boorstein, Mark McCauslin, and Derek Gullino.

PHOTOGRAPH CREDITS

WILLIAM ABRANOWICZ
132, 133

ANTHONY AMOS
16 (top)

SANG AN
12, 29 (second from top), 72, 76,
99, 112, 127, 131,135, 157, 171,
173, 175, 231 (left and middle)

JAMES BAIGRIE
104, 153, 169, 174, 226, 227
(top row)

CHRISTOPHER BAKER
5, 82, 91, 105, 106, 202

ROLAND BELLO
56, 57, 128, 181, 189

ANITA CALERO
16 (bottom left), 66, 77, 81, 85,
118, 119, 170

GEMMA COMAS
34 (top)

CRAIG CUTLER
39, 107, 111, 172, 230 (top)

BEATRIZ DA COSTA
78, 117, 158, 193

BARBARA DONNIELLI
36

JIM FRANCO
31 (third from top)

LAURIE FRANKEL
46, 69

DANA GALLAGHER
19 (bottom right), 20 (top), 30 (top),
32, 68, 70, 100, 101, 110, 122, 123,
125, 136, 139, 144, 145, 164–167,
176, 182, 190, 191, 196, 199, 231
(right), 249, 251

GENTL & HYERS
6, 15, 17, 20 (bottom left), 23 (bottom
right), 29 (third from top), 58, 61,
64, 94, 97, 116, 121, 177, 194, 220

THAYER ALLYSON GOWDY
37 (bottom right)

FRANK HECKERS
54, 217

TROY HOUSE
23 (bottom left), 53

LISA HUBBARD
29 (bottom), 31 (bottom), 67

RICK LEW
20 (bottom right), 163

JONATHAN LOVEKIN
2, 28 (bottom), 31 (top)

GEOFF LUNG
19 (top), 28 (top), 62

CHARLES MARAIA
18, 19 (bottom left), 37 (top), 230
(bottom row)

WILLIAM MEPPEM
21, 44, 83, 86, 87, 188, 232

JAMES MERRELL
192

JOHNNY MILLER
8, 11, 26, 27, 38, 50, 80, 108, 143,
156, 180, 185, 210, 213–216, 221,
222, 224, 227 (bottom row), 228,
233 (bottom row)

AMY NEUNSINGER
37 (bottom left), 141

VICTORIA PEARSON
23 (top), 30 (bottom), 34 (bottom left),
47, 48, 79, 102, 115, 124, 134, 161,
186, 205

GRANT PETERSON
31 (second from top), 130

JOSÉ MANUEL
PICAYO RIVERA
16 (bottom right), 25, 84, 93, 178, 179

MARIA ROBLEO
65

ALEXANDRA ROWLEY
155

CHARLES SCHILLER
35

VICTOR SCHRAGER
51, 52, 63, 71, 98, 126, 162

THOMAS STRAUB
22

KIRSTEN STRECKER
29 (top), 30 (second from top), 49,
88, 90, 92, 103, 120, 152, 154, 195,
218, 219

MIKKEL VANG
34 (bottom right), 129, 140, 142,
148, 151, 200, 201, 229

SIMON WATSON
30 (third from top)

WENDELL T. WEBBER
233 (top row)

ANNA WILLIAMS
55, 89, 109, 146, 147, 168, 187, 225

INDEX

A

Almond(s). See also MARZIPAN
 Cherry Cake, 178–79
 -Cornmeal Pound Cake, 234
 Dacquoise, 236
 -Hazelnut Cake, 96
 Nougat, 248
Apple Cake, 235
Applesauce Cake, 70–71
Appliqué Cake, 82

B

Bahama Orchid Cake, 53
bakers, professional, 40–42
baking strips, 207
Bamboo Wave Cake, 193
bands, chocolate, making, 230
Basket Cake, Citrus, 177
Basketweave Cake, Rustic,
 194–95
basketweave patterns, piping,
 220–21
basketweave piping tip, 217–19
Beaded Bouquet Cake, 116–17
Beautiful Berries, 15
Beehive Cake, 68–69
bench scrapers, 210
Beribboned Bouquet Cake,
 110–11
Berries, Beautiful, 15
Blooming Branches Cake,
 170–71
Blushing Dogwood Cake, 124
Bouquet Cake, Beaded, 116–17
Bouquet Cake, Beribboned,
 110–11
Branches, Blooming, Cake,
 170–71
bride and groom cake toppers,
 38–39
Brownie Cakes, Rich, 200
Bubble Cake, 106–7
Buttercream

about, 28
Caramel, 239
Chocolate, 138
Coconut, 238
Coffee, 239
-covered cakes, preparing,
 212–13
Fruit-Flavored, 239
listings and photos of, 26–27
Mint, 239
Pistachio, 96
storing, 206
Swiss Meringue, 238
Vanilla-Bean, 75
Vanilla Custard, 239
White Chocolate, 238
Buttoned-Up Cake, 56–57
Button-Topped Boxes Cake, 134

C

cake boards, 39, 206
cake rounds, 210
Cakes. See CAKES (BASIC
 RECIPES); WEDDING CAKES
Cakes (basic recipes)
 Almond-Cornmeal Pound, 234
 Almond Dacquoise, 236
 Almond-Hazelnut, 96
 Apple, 235
 bakers' guidelines, 252
 baking, tips for, 207
 buttercream, preparing,
 212–13
 Carrot, 236
 Chocolate Butter, 114
 Coconut, 60
 Devil's Food, 150
 freezing, 207
 Lemon Poppy Seed Pound,
 237
 listings and photos of, 26
 Marble, 198

Mocha Spice, 138
 Red Velvet, 184
 Vanilla-Bean Sponge, 160
 White Butter, 235
 Yellow, 74
cake table, rotating, 210
cake toppers, bride and groom,
 38–39
Calico Cake, Charming,
 146–47
Candied Orange Slices, 75
Candy Cake, Shimmering, 127
Candy Sampler Cake, 140
Candy Straw Cake, 156–57
Caramel, 248
 Buttercream, 239
 –Cream Cheese Filling, 243
 Sauce, 244
Carrot Cake, 236
Cascading Orchids Cake, 171
centerpiece cake, 37
Charlotte Cake, Ladyfinger, 64
"Charlotte" Cake, Chocolate,
 172–73
Charming Calico Cake, 146–47
Cheesecake, Cherry, 62–63
Cherry
 Almond Cake, 178–79
 Cheesecake, 62–63
 -Chocolate Ganache, 114
Cherry Blossom Cake, Pink,
 112–15
cherry blossoms, gum-paste,
 making, 227
Chestnut Chocolate Cake,
 118–19
Chocolate
 bands, making, 230
 Butter Cake, 114
 Buttercream, 138
 Cake, Megève, 120–21
 "Charlotte" Cake, 172–73

-Cherry Ganache, 114
Chestnut Cake, 118–19
decorative, about, 29
Devil's Food Cake, 150
Devil's Food Finale Cake,
 148–51
Fudge Frosting, 241
and Geranium Cake, 144–45
Glaze, Shiny, 241
Kumquat Cake, 176–77
leaves, making, 230
Marble Cake, 198
Mint Cake, 92–93
Mocha Spice Cake, 138
Modeling, 245
modeling dough, about, 28
Petal Cake, 136–39
Petals, 244
Red Velvet Cake, 184
Sauce, 150
tempering, 229
White, Buttercream, 238
White, Fondant, 240
White, Mousse, 242
White, Tower Cake, 91
wood grain (faux boix),
 making, 231
working with, 229–31
Chrysanthemum Cake, Meringue,
 130
Citrus Basket Cake, 177
Citrus Celebration Cake, 72–75
Coconut
 Buttercream, 238
 Cake, 60
 Cake, Seven-Tier, 58–61
 Crème Anglaise, 60
Coffee Buttercream, 239
Colorful Hydrangea Cake,
 102–3
compotes, about, 29
contracts, for wedding cake, 41

-Cherry Ganache, 114
Corinthian Cake, 84–85
Cornmeal-Almond Pound Cake,
 234
Cream Cheese–Caramel Filling,
 243
Cream Cheese Frosting, 184, 241
Creamware Cake, 52–53
Crème Anglaise, Coconut, 60
Crewelwork Cake, 88–89
Croquembouche
 recipe for, 247–51
 in Sweets and Sentiments
 Cakes, 164–65
cupcake tiers, 37
Cupcake Tower, Homespun,
 82–83
Cupcake Tower, Mini, 142
curd, about, 29
Curd, Lemon, 75

D

Dacquoise, Almond, 236
Daisies Cake, Delightful, 155
Daisy Garden Cake, 47
Damask Cake, 186–87
Darcy and Andy's Cake, 132–33
Delightful Daisies Cake, 155
dessert cart display, 34
Devil's Food Cake, 150
Devil's Food Finale Cake,
 148–51
Dogwood Cake, Blushing, 124
Dotted Petals Cake, 88
dowels, wooden, 210
Drifting Petals Cake, 64–65
dusting powders, 210

E

Embroidery Cake, 44
equipment, imprinting, 215
equipment glossary, 210–11
Eyelet Cake, 109

F

Farmstand Fruit and Buttercream
Cake, 166–67
Faux Bois Cake, 124–25
faux boix, chocolate, making,
231
Fillings
bakers' guidelines, 253
buttercream, about, 28
Caramel–Cream Cheese, 243
chilled curd used as, 29
compotes and preserves as, 29
ganache, about, 30
Italian Meringue, 150
Lemon Curd, 75
listings and photos of, 26–27
marzipan, about, 31
Mascarpone Cream, 243
Pastry Cream, 242
Swiss Meringue, 246
White Chocolate Mousse,
242
floral supplies, 210
Flower Hat Cake, 76
flowers
crystallized, about, 30
crystallized, preparing, 225
edible, about, 30
edible, using, 225
flower formers, 210
fresh, working with, 224
Fondant
about, 29
White Chocolate, 240
working with, 214
Fondant-covered wedding cakes
Appliqué Cake, 82
Bamboo Wave Cake, 193
Beaded Bouquet Cake,
116–17
Beehive Cake, 68–69
Beribboned Bouquet Cake,
110–11
Blooming Branches Cake,
170–71
Buttoned-Up Cake, 56–57
Button-Topped Boxes Cake,
134
Cascading Orchids Cake, 171
Charming Calico Cake,
146–47
Chocolate Mint Cake, 92–93
Corinthian Cake, 84–85

Creamware Cake, 52–53
Crewelwork Cake, 88–89
Daisy Garden Cake, 47
Damask Cake, 186–87
Darcy and Andy's Cake,
132–33
Delightful Daisies Cake, 155
Dotted Petals Cake, 88
Eyelet Cake, 109
Flower Hat Cake, 76
French Confectionary Box
Cake, 81
Garden of Sweet Delights
Cake, 152–53
Garlands and Wreaths Cake,
104
Handcrafted Hellebore Cake,
99
Ironstone Cake, 71
Ivory Dots Cake, 168
Lemon Grove Cake, 46–47
Lily-of-the-Valley Cake, 173
Lovely Licorice Cake, 174–75
Marbleized Cake, 200–201
Matelassé Cake, 54–55
Mini Cupcake Tower, 142
Paper Ornament Cake,
128–29
Patterned Nonpareil Cake,
130–31
Pearl and Shell Cake, 78–79
Perfect Pear Cake, 103
Pink Cherry Blossom Cake,
112–15
Pink Lusterware Cake, 50–51
Pink Macaroon Cake, 66–67
Playful Paper Flower Cake,
140–41
Pretty Pleats Cake, 76–77
Primrose Cake, 79
Pulled-Sugar Ribbon Cake,
107
Ribbons and Bows Cake, 181
Royal Icing Reliefs Cake, 120
Scalloped Bands and Bows
Cake, 196–99
Seven-Tier Classic Cake,
48–49
Silk-Cord Accents Cake, 128
Snow-Flecked Pinecones Cake,
190–91
Transferware Cake, 98–99

Trio of Freesia Cakes, 134–35
Trio of Shell Cakes, 117
Vintage Monogram Cake,
188–89
Wedgwood Cake, 126–27
food colors, gel-paste, 210
Freesia Cakes, Trio of, 134–35
French Confectionary Box Cake,
81
Frosting-covered wedding cakes
Bahama Orchid Cake, 53
Bubble Cake, 106–7
Chocolate and Geranium Cake,
144–45
Chocolate Chestnut Cake,
118–19
Chocolate Kumquat Cake,
176–77
Chocolate Petal Cake, 136–39
Citrus Basket Cake, 177
Citrus Celebration Cake,
72–75
Colorful Hydrangea Cake,
102–3
Devil's Food Finale Cake,
148–51
Drifting Petals Cake, 64–65
Farmstand Fruit and
Buttercream Cake, 166–67
Faux Bois Cake, 124–25
Homespun Cupcake Tower,
82–83
Megève Chocolate Cake,
120–21
Meringue Chrysanthemum
Cake, 130
Meringue Monogram Cake,
86–87
Meringue Mushrooms Cake,
100–101
Parrot-Tulip Quartet of Cakes,
168–69
Petite Piped Cakes, 90–91
Pink Madeleine Cake,
158–61
Red Velvet Cake, 182–85
Rich Brownie Cakes, 200
Robin's Egg Cake, 85
Rose Basket Cake, 63
Rose Garden Cake, 152
Ruffly Rose-Petal Garland
Cake, 174

Rustic Basketweave Cake,
194–95
Rustic Roses Cake, 163
Seven-Tier Coconut Cake,
58–61
Showered-in-White Cake,
192–93
Sugar Hydrangea Cake, 110
Sweets and Sentiments Cakes,
164–65
Tower of Roses Cake, 194
Tuscan Grapes Cake, 92
Frostings. See also Buttercream;
Glazes; Icings
bakers' guidelines, 253
Chocolate-Cherry Ganache,
114
Cream Cheese, 184, 241
Fudge, 241
ganache, about, 30
Italian Meringue, 150
listings and photos of, 26–27
Seven-Minute, 240
Swiss Meringue, 246
Fruit, Farmstand, and
Buttercream Cake, 166–67
Fruit-Flavored Buttercream,
239
fruits, decorating cake with, 30
Fudge Frosting, 241

G

ganache, about, 30
Ganache, Chocolate-Cherry, 114
Garden of Sweet Delights Cake,
152–53
Garlands and Wreaths Cake, 104
gel-paste food colors, 210
Geranium and Chocolate Cake,
144–45
"gift" table display, 34
Ginger-Infused Simple Syrup,
245
Glazes
about, 29
Chocolate, Shiny, 241
warm curd used as, 29
glossary, equipment, 210–11
glossary, imprinting, 215
glossary, piping, 217, 223
golden trimmings display, 34
Grapes Cake, Tuscan, 92

groom and bride cake toppers,
38–39
groom's cake, 43
gum paste
about, 30
tools, 210
working with, 226–27

H

Handcrafted Hellebore Cake, 99
Hazelnut-Almond Cake, 96
Hellebore Cake, Handcrafted, 99
Homespun Cupcake Tower,
82–83
Hydrangea Cake, Colorful, 102–3
Hydrangea Cake, Sugar, 110

I

icing damask, preparing, 233
Icings. See also GLAZES
choosing or buying, 206
Italian Meringue, 150
Italian meringue, about, 31
Royal, 243
royal, about, 31
Swiss Meringue, 246
Swiss meringue, about, 31
imprinting glossary, 215
Ironstone Cake, 71
Ivory Dots Cake, 168

K

knife, serrated, 210
Kumquat Chocolate Cake,
176–77

L

lace canopy display, 34, 35
Ladyfinger Charlotte Cake, 64
leaf piping tip, 217–19
leaves, chocolate, making, 230
Lemon
Curd, 75
Grove Cake, 46–47
and Latticework Cake,
154–55
Madeleines, 246–47
Poppy Seed Pound Cake, 237
Simple Syrup, 75
Licorice Cake, Lovely, 174–75
Lily-of-the-Valley Cake, 173
Lovely Licorice Cake, 174–75

M

Macaroon Cake, Pink, 66–67
Madeleine Cake, Pink, 158–61
Madeleines, Lemon, 246–47
Marble Cake, 198
Marbleized Cake, 200–201
marbleized transfer sheets, 229
Marzipan
    about, 31
    in Cherry Almond Cake,
        178–79
    in Perfect Pear Cake, 103
    recipe for, 243
    in Stately Springerle Cake,
        144
    in Treasures of the Woods
        Cake, 122–23
    in Woodland Nut Cake,
        94–97
    working with, 228
Mascarpone Cream Filling,
    243
Matelassé Cake, 54–55
Megève Chocolate Cake,
    120–21
Meringue
    Bouquet Cake, 202
    Chrysanthemum Cake, 130
    Disks, 245
    Italian, about, 31
    Italian (recipe), 150
    Monogram Cake, 86–87
    Mushrooms, 246
    mushrooms, preparing, 233
    Mushrooms Cake, 100–101
    Simple, 245
    Swiss, about, 31
    Swiss, Buttercream, 238
    Swiss (recipe), 246
mini cakes, 37
Mini Cupcake Tower, 142
Mint Buttercream, 239
Mint Chocolate Cake, 92–93
Mocha Spice Cake, 138
Modeling Chocolate, 245
modeling dough, chocolate, 28
Monogram Cake, Meringue,
    86–87
Monogram Cake, Vintage,
    188–89
monogram design, transferring,
    232
monograms, piping, 217

Mousse, Passion-Fruit, 248
Mousse, White Chocolate, 242

N

namesake cakes, 36, 37
Nonpareil Cake, Patterned,
    130–31
Nougat, 248
Nut(s). See also ALMOND(s);
    MARZIPAN
    Almond-Hazelnut Cake, 96
    Cake, Woodland, 94–97
    Chocolate Chestnut Cake,
        118–19
    Pistachio Buttercream, 96

O

Orange(s)
    Citrus Celebration Cake,
        72–75
    Slices, Candied, 75
Orchids, Cascading, Cake, 171
oversize piping tip, 217–19

P

Paper Ornament Cake, 128–29
Parrot-Tulip Quartet of Cakes,
    168–69
Passion-Fruit Mousse, 248
pastillage, about, 31
pastry bags and tips, 210
pastry brushes, 210
Pastry Cream, 242
Patterned Nonpareil Cake,
    130–31
Pear Cake, Perfect, 103
Pearl and Shell Cake, 78–79
Perfect Pear Cake, 103
petal piping tip, 217–19
Petals, Chocolate, 244
Petite Piped Cakes, 90–91
Picket Fence Cake, 104–5
Pinecones, Snow-Flecked, Cake,
    190–91
Pink Cherry Blossom Cake,
    112–15
Pink Lusterware Cake, 50–51
Pink Macaroon Cake, 66–67
Pink Madeleine Cake, 158–61
Pin Tucks and Ruffles Cake, 189
piping 101, 216–23
Pistachio Buttercream, 96

pizza wheel, 210
Playful Paper Flower Cake,
    140–41
Poppy Seed Lemon Pound Cake,
    237
Pound Cake, Almond-Cornmeal,
    234
Pound Cake, Lemon Poppy Seed,
    237
preserves, about, 29
Pretty Piped Bows Cake, 67
Pretty Pleats Cake, 76–77
Primrose Cake, 79
Pulled-Sugar Ribbon Cake, 107

R

Red Velvet Cake, 182–85
Ribbon Cake, Pulled-Sugar, 107
Ribbons and Bows Cake, 181
Rich Brownie Cakes, 200
Robin's Egg Cake, 85
rolling pins, 210
rose, gum-paste, making, 226
rose, piping, 220
Rose Basket Cake, 63
Rose Garden Cake, 152
Rose-Petal Garland Cake, Ruffly,
    174
Roses, Tower of, Cake, 194
Roses Cake, Rustic, 163
Rose Topper Cake, 12
round (plain) piping tip, 217–19
Royal Icing, 243
royal icing, about, 31
Royal Icing Reliefs Cake, 120
Ruffly Rose-Petal Garland Cake,
    174
Rustic Basketweave Cake,
    194–95
Rustic Roses Cake, 163

S

Sauces
    Caramel, 244
    Chocolate, 150
    Coconut Crème Anglaise, 60
Scalloped Bands and Bows Cake,
    196–99
Seven-Minute Frosting, 240
Seven-Tier Classic Cake, 48–49
Seven-Tier Coconut Cake, 58–61
Shell Cakes, Trio of, 117

Shimmering Candy Cake, 127
Shortcake, Strawberry, 166
Showered-in-White Cake,
    192–93
Silk-Cord Accents Cake, 128
Simple Syrup, Ginger-Infused,
    245
Simple Syrup, Lemon, 75
Snow-Flecked Pinecones Cake,
    190–91
spatula, metal, 210
spatula, silicone, 210
Springerle Cake, Stately, 144
Spun Sugar, 249, 250
star piping tips, 217–19
Stately Springerle Cake, 144
Strawberry Shortcake, 166
Sugar Hydrangea Cake, 110
sugar paste. See GUM PASTE
Sweeping Monograms Cake, 54
Sweets and Sentiments Cakes,
    164–65

T

Tower of Roses Cake, 194
Tower of Truffles Cake, 68
Transferware Cake, 98–99
Treasures of the Woods Cake,
    122–23
trimmings, buying, 206
Trio of Freesia Cakes, 134–35
Trio of Shell Cakes, 117
Truffles, Tower of, Cake, 68
Tuile Banners
    recipe for, 249, 250
    in Sweets and Sentiments
        Cakes, 164–65
tulip, gum-paste, making, 227
Tuscan Grapes Cake, 92

V

Vanilla-Bean Buttercream, 75
Vanilla-Bean Sponge Cake, 160
Vanilla Custard Buttercream,
    239
Vintage Monogram Cake,
    188–89

W

Wedding Band Cake, 162–63
wedding cakes
    assembling, 208

baking cake layers for, 207
budgeting for, 42
color motifs for, 22, 23
components of, 24–27
cost-saving considerations, 42
decorating, 208
design, choosing, 206
displaying, 33–39
equipment glossary, 210–11
fabric motifs for, 23
fall season style, 19
finding inspiration for, 14
floral motifs for, 23
fruit motifs for, 23
garden-themed, 20, 21
groom's cake, 43
icings and trimmings for,
    28–31
international traditions, 43
modern style, 16
planning tips, 204–9
rustic style, 16
seaside-themed, 20
spring season style, 18, 19
summer season style, 19
traditional style, 16, 17
transporting, 209
tropical-themed, 20
wedding location
    considerations, 20–21
wedding style considerations,
    16–17
whimsical style, 16
winter season style, 19
woodland-themed, 20
working with baking
    professionals, 40–42
Wedgwood Cake, 126–27
White Butter Cake, 235
White Chocolate
    Buttercream, 238
    Fondant, 240
    Mousse, 242
    Tower Cake, 91
wooden dowels, 210
wood grain (faux boix), chocolate,
    making, 231
Woodland Nut Cake, 94–97

Y

Yellow Cake, 74